FACEBOOK MARKETING

Step by Step Facebook Secrets to Connect, Engage, Grow, Influence, and Sell

By

David James Miles

TABLE OF CONTENTS

DESCRIPTION

In a vast ocean of 1.28 billion daily active users and 60 million businesses, you need to be able to stand out from the crowd if you want to do marketing effectively on Facebook.

They must be helpful and you must act thoughtfully. In order to master Facebook marketing, it is important to apply the inbound philosophy.

Luckily, Facebook tools focus on marketers who want to build an authentic relationship with their audience. With the impressive collection of analytics tools that Facebook offers, you can get to know your audience before you publish content. With the growing number of multimedia content options that Facebook offers, you can explore new creative paths, and the page statistics give you an insight into the content your visitors interact with. So, you can also segment your advertising so that it is helpful and not intrusive.

Your fans allow you to access them via Facebook. With the tips in this guide, you should have all the tools at your fingertips to get the most out of this opportunity.

INTRODUCTION

Facebook is enormous. As the greatest person to person communication site on the planet, it has more than 2.20 billion powerful customers, 66% of whom sign in consistently.

Facebook went from being dark, scarcely 10 years earlier, to having billions of people using it day by day. Will Facebook be bound to disappointment like other web-based life destinations before? I think not. Facebook is diving in for the whole deal.

Additionally, with such an extensive customer base, sitting above Facebook genuinely is certainly not a brilliant thought, particularly on the off chance that you are not kidding about internet showcasing. You can focus on your optimal market utilizing Facebook relentlessly. The examination is: how might you acquire customers with your promotions with Facebook?

Luckily the Facebook elevating stage empowers you to focus in and demonstrate the sort of people you're hunting down. You can center by territory, economics, interests, and fundamentally more.

In this guide, I'll exhibit to you the basics of for the most part acknowledged strategies to use Facebook, further boosting your leverage. The guide is for the fast student who needs an opening to exhibiting their business on the world's greatest web-based life webpage.

CHAPTER 1

WHO'S ON FACEBOOK?

Facebook may have started as a casual network for students, however regardless, now, about everyone with a site is using it.

The base age essential is 13, and there is inspiration to believe it as is being utilized by all other age gatherings.

Facebook doesn't transparently release data on their most unmistakable age gatherings, yet an examination by Pew showed that individual to individual correspondence is most predominant with the 18-29 age gatherings. Its unmistakable quality lessens with age. It is likewise utilized by those in the 65 or more gatherings.

I can promise you that, paying little respect to what age bunch you're focusing; there will be all that anyone could need customers to go around on Facebook.

By what method Might You Market on Facebook?

Facebook has three instruments (pages, advertisements, and parties) that can be utilized by anybody. These decisions have its own one of a kind markets and they can be joined for progressively noteworthy reach for your client needs.

Pages

Facebook pages take after profiles, for affiliations, affiliations, and open figures markets.

Customers can "Like" a page, which infers they'll normally get invigorates from that page in their news channel. In any case, with the true objective to see the posts each time they are incorporated, you need to tap the choice to see posts first. Something different of significance, it's believable you won't see the updates in light of the way that Facebook needs Pages to help (consume money) presents for more prominent reach on clients.

Clients furthermore have the decision to "Like" a page anyway not tail it. (Customers moreover can seek after a couple of profiles on the off chance that they wish).

Blocks: It can be hard to get a strong balance and assembling a fan base with a page.

Advancements

Facebook offers a magnificent spotlight on publicizing.

You can make advancements centered at express geographic districts, ages, guidance levels, and even the sorts of contraptions used for checking. Facebook similarly allows customers to conceal advancements they couldn't care less for and "Like" a page proper underneath an advertisement.

Ideal conditions: Ads have mind blowing concentrating on target customers.

Burdens: Ads can get expensive, dependent upon your targets.

Get-togethers

Facebook bunches resemble talk social affairs. Anyway with additional features that show pages and profiles you can utilize these gatherings furthering your potential benefit or even make one yourself (like a course of occasions). You can make a gathering related to your industry or thing commitments as a way to deal with contact potential customers.

Good conditions: Groups are free and have raised measures of responsibility.

Weaknesses: Groups can be very dull and requesting to upkeep.

The Most Effective Method To Market With Pages

Facebook pages are the most clear and least requesting way to deal with start showcasing with Facebook.

To utilize the site is free, by and large easy to set up (at any rate in their basic structures), and incredibly versatile. There are for all intents and purposes no downsides, either. Tragically, various associations don't use Facebook to their most extreme limit, or all the more terrible, use them incapably. The principles spread out in this book will empower you to refrain from submitting those blunders.

Profile Photo and Cover Image

Your profile photograph should be your logo, essential as that. The spread picture is a substitute story. It's really dependent upon you to pick what to put here. Some utilization photographs of operators, while others utilize sumptuous HD premium photographs and put their contact data in the spread picture. Pick a photograph that will refresh your page and draw the eye of your guests.

"About" Section

The "About" area ought to be put legitimately underneath your business logo. This is your opportunity to support anybody visiting your page what your business offers.

Guarantee you put incredible data here, telling people what you're association does, for what reason you're exceptional, and other intriguing focal points. Put aside an opportunity to create this region expressly for your Facebook social event of individuals.

You can copy the substance from the "About" page of your website or blog on the off chance that you don't know what to put. Make a point to fill in most of your data under "Fundamental Info." Keep it well perfect and easygoing. An agreeable tone when in doubt works best on Facebook. You in like manner may need to put your place of work in this segment in the event that you have a physical store area.

Post Useful Information to Your Timeline

What you post to your course of events, what your put will show up in the news channels of everyone who has "Preferred" your page, comparatively as it does when you present something all alone profile.

Thusly, ensure what you're appearing beneficial and attracts on your supporters. Take the necessary steps not to post vast updates about a similar thing, and don't post endless pointless data that doesn't take into account your devotees either.

Here are a couple of contemplations for the sorts of things you should post to your page:

Connections to articles related to your association or your industry.

Connections to your blog passages.

Coupon codes for fans to get a decent arrangement on your things.

New Thing Assertions

Make associations with your fans that they may find as profitable. Yet again, guarantee that your posts are prized. Moreover, don't post over and over consistently, with the exception of if there's an extraordinary event going on, or something new of significance to them.

Ask Your Fans Inquiries

Getting your fans to favor your page is an extraordinary strategy to mix certainty and get them to confide in you, and consider you to be an innovator in your field.

What you ask depends, all things considered, on your thing and your claim to fame, yet asking open-request as a rule accumulates the best responses.

Posing inquiries on another thing thought or undertaking, can be a not too bad technique to influence your fans that your association contemplates what they need. Getting more prominent duty on a post may moreover empower you to accomplish the most elevated purpose of the Facebook News Feed.

Do whatever it takes not to Spam

Spam is one of the quickest approaches to lose fans. If you don't effectively disturb them, yet pass on constrained time blurbs about your association, while never including anything of critical worth, by then you will encounter impressive challenges getting and keeping fans. Before you post anything, ask concerning whether it really builds the estimation of the talk. If not, don't send it.

Concentrate Your Statistics and Results

Facebook Insights offers some amazingly phenomenal request for pages. Concentrate on them. For instance, say you see a noteworthy flood in fans (or a drop off), see what you've posted starting late, and check whether you can comprehend a clarification behind the example. By at that point, post an increasingly conspicuous proportion of that sort of material (or less, in case you're losing fans).

Coordinated Advertising

Facebook publicizing gathers so much measurable information about its customers, that it has an extraordinary reputation among other online networking showcasing destinations on the web.

You can target customers reliant on for all intents and purposes anything you may find in their profiles, and moreover track your prosperity with every amount.

Advancements can be continued running on for each impression or per-click premise. Facebook exhibits to your supporters what offers are for advancements like yours, so you know whether your offer is, as per others in your industry. You similarly can set step by step following so there's no risk of blowing your money related arrangement for advertisements.

Assortments of Facebook Ads

There are various advancements you can do with Facebook. You can make progressions that direct to your Facebook page, or to a site not on Facebook. You can make advancements to push a Facebook occasion, total with a RSVP partner. You can make headways for conservative application presents and application duty.

Customers Can Hide Your Ad

Facebook used to offer the decision to "Like" any advertisement on Facebook. No more. People can "Like" a post (if it's that type) or conceal the advancement. In the wake of closing an advancement, Facebook approaches the customer to decide for what reason they couldn't have cared less for it. It's beneficial information, giving comprehension into why your advancements presumably won't do.

Change Your Ads

The extremely phenomenal thing about Facebook advertisements is that you can concentrate on advancements that can make unmistakable promotions for different gatherings. Remaining better-centered around promotions will gather better results.

For instance, you're focusing on football fans; you may make ads for various social affairs. You could have one progression explicitly accomplished for NFL fans, one at Seattle Seahawks fans, and another at Raiders fans, and a brief span later have those advancements introduced just to individuals who have showed up for football, further boosting your favorable position to admirers of those gatherings.

Of course, assume you've concentrated on people reliant on their reverence for a particular book. You could determine that book in the advancement itself, to make it bound to snatch their eye. Make assorted advancements for different books, and after that objective as necessities be.

Facebook isn't just earth shattering. It's versatile. Despite what sort of association you run, it has enough special publicizing options that you can tailor your displaying tries to oblige your association, your money related arrangement, and your time goals.

To be sure, it can set aside some chance to turn out to be progressively familiar with most of its features, anyway it's worthy, in spite of a little work on your part. Facebook still is creating at a speedy pace, and reliably it transforms into a progressively essential bit of online business with internet based life advertising.

It's moreover indispensable to capitalize on current chances. For the event, organizations that are insightful about Facebook advertisements still value an early-adopter advantage.

Once more standard sponsors start advancing into space, competition will manufacture, publicizing costs will rise, and customers will end up being much pickier. In case Facebook is unquestionably not a present bit of your promoting exertion, it should be. Set aside some an opportunity to pick up a chance to develop your business, start a few promotions, and see what occurs.

Every one of these procedures work in Facebook, however you simply need to become acclimated to rehearsing how things work, when you do it, at that point it turns out to be anything but difficult to do, your business will soar.

CHAPTER 2

WHY USE SOCIAL MEDIA FOR BUSINESS

Currently you may be selling one of the most wonderful products on the marketplace today, you could really connect as well as assist the world. Nevertheless, having the most effective item doesn't mean that individuals will be able know about it or what it is you created. You may be making no sales whatsoever. You don't have the ideal knowledge of advertising and marketing, and also this equates to no person seeing your item or what solutions you are using. To complete this, you require to recognize how to arrangement promos and also marketing campaigns.

With all that stated, you can't just advertise anywhere nowadays, publications, papers and craigslist isn't going to do it. The internet is the future, and it will certainly be a matter of time when all old approaches of promoting your service will not function, actually it does not function, with online engulfing the past, we are building business of the future with social media sites advertising and marketing. This isn't ruin as well as grief, it merely suggests out with the old as well as in with the brand-new.

There is the disagreement that the items you are offering are not distinct, as others are marketing it too, so exactly how does one go about scaling up their business in spite of the competition? That is where social networks advertising comes into play, the ones with the same products as you, are making even more cash due to the fact that these organization recognize just how to make use of platforms as well as social media sites to their benefit.

It does not matter if you are the stay at residence mommy with an on-line service, or you have a real stroll in shop, you require to create a brand name, and also online character, a visibility. And also, exactly how you do this, is with social networks advertising.

Social media site is extra prominent than ever, as well as when it involves marketing, it's a wonderful way to take your company to the next level. A lot has been stated about social media sites advertising and marketing, but allows take a look at the advantages and also advantages that Facebook can offer your organization.

Enhanced Item Recognition

When we talk of developing your brand as well as obtaining customers to enjoy your item, social media sites is the most effective device for the task; you can raise your organizations prominence and dominate the competitors in no time. And also, not only this, you will also be standing up as well as close with what consumers are looking for, what you are using, and placing you ahead of the competition.

Building Brand Name Loyalty

If you wish to remain in business for the long term, then you require to have a follower base, where customers are seeking you out as the "most likely to" for all their buying demands. Having routine sales is a wonderful perk, but with no strong base of consumers, you can promptly sink. Facebook advertising and marketing can unlock to success in your business, permitting you to obtain more in contact with customers on an individual degree, being familiar with what they desire, as well as this response can aid your service greatly. Ever ask yourself why when you stroll into Starbucks' that the barista asks for your name? This is since Howard Shultz the owner carried out a method of developing a devoted client base, by engaging them to find back as well as really feel welcome.

Expense Effectiveness

Using the old approaches of marketing your business can leave you with substantial responsibility. Social media site marketing is really inexpensive and powerful.

All you require is a desktop or laptop and also internet Wi-Fi. As your business remains to expand, it just makes good sense to cut costs, using social media sites to promote your items is a budget-friendly method.

Coming to be an Authority

Keeping the consumer satisfied as well as producing loyalty of your brand name is terrific at creating an on the internet identity for your company. You begin to get viewed as the authority on the product you are offering. This is where interaction is so essential.

With raised presence of your product throughout the various social media sites internet sites as well as involving with prospective clients, you appear much more trustworthy than other services. When others see that you are reacting to customers in a genuine means, then this possible clientele sees you as down-to-earth, and that you truly take care of the client. When you put in the effort with social networks advertisements, you have an online identity, a person that individuals look up to, and also this can result in others advertising your items indirectly for you.

Advantages of Social Media Advertising and Marketing

The advantages have actually been clear so far, if you possess an organization and haven't capitalized on social media sites, after that you need to take it to the next level. Discover how to develop profiles, get all your service information up and also ready online, create a character, a brand name, and also build a faithful client base. These approaches and also even more will certainly be showing up in the following phases in a very easy to follow format. Come to be a victor as well as pro at social networks advertising and marketing as well as Facebook ads. Dominate the competitors.

CHAPTER 3

CREATING A FACEBOOK PAGE FOR YOUR BUSINESS

What is Facebook Business Manager?

The Facebook Business Manager is used for managing your pages and ad accounts. You can also control access to them since you may view the people who can take hold of them and change their permissions if need be. Furthermore, you can work with agencies or give them your account if you want them to manage your ad campaigns.

Before you begin advertising on Facebook, therefore, you need to create a Business Manager account. To set up, you have to do the following.

- Visit www.facebook.com/business.

- Click on the right-hand corner and select "Create a Page."

- This action will take you to a page where you'll see "Business or Brand" and "Community or Public Figure." Choose the one that your audience is most likely to remember when thinking about your business.

- After choosing your type of business, you'll have to fill in your page name. Then, a list of categories will come up under the category option. Take a pick and read through Facebook's terms and conditions for Business Pages. Click "Accept" if you're okay with the legalities to get started.

- Next, add photos to your page. You can use your logo or any picture that represents your brand or conveys its personality as your cover image. However, ensure to use a high-quality picture and include ones that are watermarked with our business name to create good first impressions. Your image shouldn't be less than 150 pixels tall and 400 pixels wide.

- Add a description of your products using no more than 155 characters. Seize this opportunity to let people know about your business, as well as to make it attractive to viewers. Your customers should be your primary focus, so share only what they need to know as clearly as possible. Keep your post short and simple. Click "Save" when you're done with this.

- Create your vanity URL (a.k.a. username). People should know how to find you on Facebook through it. Your username should not exceed 50 characters. Make sure that it can be easily remembered as well. In truth, using your business name is advisable to make things easy. Click on "Create Username" when you've made a decision, and a box will show you links through which people can connect with your business. Click "Continue" to keep filling in your details.

- Place a written background of the business in the "About" section on the left-hand side of your page. Enter all details including your contact information, other social media accounts, price range, and working hours. This way, if a customer is looking for a particular product, they will focus on the price range and won't bother to contact you until they are ready to buy. Click "Continue" when done with this.

Now, your page is ready for your first post. Ensure you share an engaging and valuable content before inviting people to like your page so that they will keep on visiting it.

Nevertheless, posting content is one thing; engaging with your audience is another. Invite family and friends to hit the "Like" button and possibly post positive reviews about the business. Promote your Page through other channels like Twitter, Instagram or your website. You might have come across some posts on Twitter that goes like "Follow us at [vanity URL]", and you can do the same thing.

How to Improve or Optimize Your Facebook Page

Your Facebook page is ready, and now you're thinking of the best ways to optimize it to increase engagement and meet advertising objectives or goals. Doing the following will help you optimize your page.

Add a Pinned Post on Your Page

A Pinned Post should be added at the top of your Facebook page, under your cover photo. It can show your visitors important information such as top content or promotions. The position of a pinned post makes it be seen by your visitors and entices them to engage with it.

To pin a post on your page, click the ellipsis on the post you want to use and find "Pin to Top of Page" on the drop-down menu that will pop up. A blue icon will appear on its top-right corner to show that your post has been pinned.

Make Good Use of Additional Tabs

There are tabs on the top-left side of your page where you'll find photos and the "About" section. Make your page unique by adding other tabs that will leave your users with an unforgettable experience. You can use the help of a developer to create custom tabs if you have over 2,000 people following you.

Add a Call-to-Action (CTA) Button

Lots of people will visit your page for different reasons, and providing them all with the necessary information might become cumbersome. You need to add the Facebook's built-in call-to-action (CTA) button then to give visitors instructions on what they can do with your offerings. E.g., Download, Shop Now, Sign Up, Watch the video, Learn More, and so on.

To add your CTA button, select the "Edit" button on your Facebook page and look for the action phrase that you'd like to use. Choose the particular message that you want to appear on the button as well. Click "Next" to see other options that you may need to decide on. Click "Finish" once you're done, and your CTA will appear on your Facebook page.

Monitor and Improve Your Page Insights

Your Page Insights will help you gather more information on how your followers interact with the content you publish, as well as your page's performance as a whole. You will be able to see the number of people who click on your CTA button, address, website or phone number. When you have access to this data, you'll be able to work towards satisfying the needs of more subscribers.

Add a Link to Your Facebook Page at the Bottom of Your Blog Post

The link you add at the bottom of your blog post is called a backlink. It gives your Facebook page more credibility and may help optimize your search engine rankings.

To create a backlink, paste the link to your page at the end of the website or article. Permit others to include your URL when sharing your posts to increase your visitor count as well.

Like Pages That are Relevant to Your Business

When you like pages that share the same location as your physical store or other products related to yours (not your competitors please!), you tend to help build a community and provide your audience with additional stuff they may need. For instance, you can invite your followers to like a make-up training tutorial page by featuring the shop on yours. You can also highlight a paint shop near you as a professional painter. To do this, click the three dots below your cover photo, select "Like as Your Page" to like the other business, and submit.

Check Your Settings Again

You should check your settings regularly, especially when the number of your followers increase, and you know if you need to adjust your preferences and requirements. Your settings should be optimized based on how you wish to interact with them. You can choose an administrator aside from yourself who can manage your Facebook Page.

How to Grow Your Personal Brand on Facebook in 2019

The above quotation says a lot about why you should have a personal brand on Facebook. After all, it will determine how you engage with your target market and the success of your business. It will also help you realize the loyalty of your subscribers.

Followers look for a good personality and an expert behind brands to promote positive communication and relationships. When you build a personal brand, your business will not suffer as people have trust in you. Growing it is the first thing you should do before creating your corporate brand.

Below is a guide on how to expand your personal brand.

Know your audience and interact with them

How do you recognize your audience and their needs? As stated earlier, your market consists of people who want or have an interest in your products or services. They will point out their necessities through interaction and allow you to supply them based on trust. They have your interest at heart and want your brand to grow. By interacting with them, you know what to and not to post on your page.

Watch out for their friends and colleagues, as well as the pages and groups that they follow. Check out the post and content they share, too. The Facebook events, conferences or webinars that these people visit can also let you know what your brand can offer to them.

Follow and make relevant comments on the pages of influencers and top bloggers in your niche; pay attention to how they write and communicate with their audiences. In addition, know why you want to grow your personal brand, whom to follow, what to write, newsletters to subscribe to, and groups to join.

Use a good profile picture

Use a high-quality cover photo to stand out and make a good impression. Your profile picture should be decent enough to depict professionalism as well.

Put your profile information and make it as detailed as possible. That's who folks can understand who you are and what your vision, personality or expertise are.

The "About" section should be completed to ensure that people can contact you or see more of your work. You can also add a link to your website, LinkedIn or Instagram at the bottom of the section. Update your status regularly and share posts to remain relevant and keep your readers coming back for more.

Set your privacy settings

To attract more followers, make your posts visible to the public. To post some private information, set it to "Friends" only. Turn off the tagging feature to avoid spam and malicious attacks.

Write with others in mind

Remember that your audience follows your views and expects you to show care and attention to what you share. Comment in simple English, be polite, stay true to promises, apologize for mistakes, follow your guts, and be humorous when appropriate.

Start a new group or page

With a new group and page, you will be able to build a community for like-minded people who will support your business and attract others in the same industry. If you have a good number of Facebook friends, you can start a group and watch it expand.

Have a username or vanity URL for branding purposes

Your username is similar to your domain name, in the sense that it makes your brand easily accessible to everyone. For instance, if you are Victor Rice, your username can be www.facebook.com/victorrice (or victorrice@gmail.com if you use email).

Share relevant content regularly

Make your opinions known through your updates on current event and happenings. Post articles according to the kind of image you want to create for yourself and the message your users will want to hear from you.

Link your Facebook page to other social networks

To raise interest in yourself and your business, link your Facebook page to other social networks such as Instagram, Twitter or personal blog. As more and more people visit these sites to read your articles, your personal brand becomes stronger. Ensure that the channels you link fit into your brand vision and that the contents are in line with your strategy.

Promote others' events on your page

Promoting an event hosted by someone in the same industry or peer group will attract new users to your page. As soon as you set the event, ensure to post updates about it often and interact with the attendees. You will be more respected and trusted if you keep doing so and invariably help you increase your target audience and sales.

Write and share diverse articles

When you post one type of article all the time, your followers may get bored. As humans, we always crave for something new and interesting. Thus, you need to broaden your scope by sharing articles from other sources (after getting permission, of course). You may add videos and images or throw questions here and there as well to keep them engaged.

Be generous

People appreciate you more when you give them something they need at a particular time. Because of that, give as much advice, information or even hacks as you can. People will always remember you for this and help promote your brand at any given opportunity.

Ask engaging questions

Find an opportunity to ask questions to your audience. This way, you can easily spark discussion and keep your brand relevant. Asking questions is also another way to build relationships among your followers when they respond with a different or same point of view.

Be responsive

You have to be responsive and engaging to grow your network of connections and personal brand. Chip in your opinion when you should and avoid being a wishful lurker. Don't be scared of making a meaningful contribution to a discussion when you have something important to add.

Keep track of your name and brand

Just like tagging someone, different kinds of alerts are being set by businesses for searches that relate to their products or brands. These alerts will let them know when a person posts content that either connects to theirs or has their brand name in it. You can add keywords that your target market often use to avoid missing out on opportunities as well.

Share the story behind your brand

People love to be motivated and sharing your brand story will do just that. You can share the story that motivated you to start your brand along with the lessons it taught you. This will make them learn from it, too, and you can encourage them to get closer to your brand.

Display your skills

Show people what you know best through your portfolio. For instance, as an ebook writer, you can display links some of your works in your portfolio.

Avoid spamming

Do not be tempted to spam - as others do - on Facebook. Sometimes you will see unrecognized links at the middle of some people's comments or some viral content in your timeline posted by spammers. You may also notice people posting the same content with different URLs. These are all examples of spamming.

Run weekly or monthly contests

You can run weekly or monthly contests to make your viewers come back for more. Offer prizes to winners so that people may show interest in future games and tell others about it. Promoting the contest on other social networks is not a bad idea either.

Take clues from successful brands
Learn from bigger brands in your niche on how they promote their brand on Facebook. Do this by following them, studying and understanding their strategies, and applying similar ideas to your campaign.

CHAPTER 4

YOUR IMAGE

It is likely that you have uploaded some basic imagery for your page upon creating your site. Now, it is time to really nail down your "look" and master it. When you are building or expanding your online presence, it is essential that you get it properly. Having a poor quality image that does not look visually appealing and can greatly inhibit your success because it prevents people from wanting to look at your content. Remember, social media has been around for a while now which has allowed marketers to set the bar pretty high. While it certainly runs by achievable high standards, you do have to do more than simply throwing up a basic image and calling it a day. Everything needs to look a specific way to attract your audience and encourage them to follow and engage with your site.

Here is what you need to do to create a custom image that attracts your target audience.

Find Your Edge

Before you really dig into creating your image, it is a good idea to find your edge. This requires you to take a look at your competition and see what they are doing on Facebook. Take some time to identify what their theme is, what color scheme they are using, and how it is helping them interact with your shared audience. You may begin to notice a trend of what color schemes and themes seem to work best with your audience. When you do notice this trend, use it to help you identify your own way of fitting into the marketplace.

The key to finding your edge is knowing what everyone else is doing and then doing it better. You want to see what is helping others succeed and then customize your own theme and color scheme that looks and performs better than anyone else's. When you do this, you begin to create a unique look that supports you in having a greater impact on reaching your target audience. When they see why you are different and better, they are more interested in following you.

Get A Logo and Cover Art Made

Facebook allows you to have a profile picture and cover art. While you can easily throw up any image, having branded images looks infinitely better. You can make this yourself, but it is recommended that you leave it to a graphic designer. Having an image that is attractive and that accurately represents your business is important. Facebook's sizing differences between mobile and desktop can sometimes make images blurry, so having a professional create your images can save you a headache and give you the opportunity to have great imagery that looks high quality as well. Remember, blurry, pixelated, or otherwise low-quality photographs will not suffice in online marketing in the 21st century.

Great places to hire professional graphic designers for a reasonable fee include Upwork, Fiverr, and 99 designs. Websites like Upwork and Fiverr will typically only charge around $5-$10 per image which makes them incredibly affordable. 99 designs do cost quite a bit more, but they also give you many options to choose from and tend to have higher quality imagery. You should choose the one that best fits your budget and needs.

Creating an Attractive Profile

Creating an attractive profile requires two things: static content that is consistent and high quality, and posts that are consistent and high quality. You want to maintain the same color palette and theme throughout your whole page. While not every single picture you post may be rooted in your color scheme, it should make sense to your overall theme and look attractive on the page that you are creating.

Pay attention to how you are posting, what you are posting, and how it all fits with what you are sharing overall. If anything does not make sense or does not amplify or enhance the overall aesthetic, theme, and message of your page, then you should refrain from posting it. Staying higher quality and trendy is important because it ensures that people enjoy scrolling your page and are more likely to follow you and revisit your page on a regular basis.

Where to Find Images for Posting

Finding images to post on your page can sometimes be challenging. However, it does not have to be. There are a few things that you need to know, however. The first thing is that you should be seeking images that are free of copyright. Royalty-free stock images are a great place to start because they provide you with great, high-quality images that you do not have to credit anyone for when you are using them. Plus, you do not have to worry about copyright infringement! Websites like Pixabay or Unsplash are great ones to go to for searching what images you want to use on your page. You can easily save the images and share them on your page with whatever caption and content you desire. Additionally, you can easily search for images that suit your theme and color scheme, so that they stay on-brand and keep your page looking beautiful and attractive to your audience.

A Word about Copyright

It is extremely important that you are cautious about copyright laws and refrain from using any image that features some form of copyright on it. If you find an image and are unsure about the copyright law behind it, refrain from using it. Using images with copyright can lead to lawsuits that are costly and that ultimately damage your business's reputation and your bottom line. It is much safer and easier to refrain from using them at all and keeping yourself protected and professional. Any image marketed as "royalty free" means that the image does not have any copyright law attached to it that requires you to credit or pay the artist. This means that you will not have to worry about copyright infringement and you can use the image as you please. There are hundreds of thousands of stock images online, so you can easily find new ones without having to reuse old ones. Plus, more are regularly being updated to popular sites like the aforementioned ones, Pixabay and Unsplash, on a daily basis!

CHAPTER 5

COMPONENTS OF FACEBOOK MARKETING

Regardless of the size of the company, Facebook is now part of the marketing strategy of most businesses. Although popular and used by many, many marketers fail to fully utilize all the features Facebook offers to create brilliant marketing campaigns. This means that both entrepreneurs and marketers need to understand the different strategies and methods that contribute to creating a positive ROI, or return on investment. This chapter describes the different components of marketing on Facebook and the practical steps to implement them. The main components of marketing on Facebook are:

- Facebook page optimization

- Facebook groups

- Social sharing on Facebook

- Visibility of your posts

- When and how often to send

- Paid options

- Best practices for advertising on Facebook

Facebook Page Optimization

Your Facebook page is the starting point for all your Facebook marketing efforts. It would be ideal if it were evaluated on both Google and Facebook so your customers and potential customers can easily find your brand. Once they have found your page, people should like the page. Here are some things you can do to optimize your site for the purposes mentioned above:

Choose a username that is meaningful and memorable

This type of URL is called a vanity URL. The web address of your Facebook page is your username for your Facebook page (e.g., www.facebook.com/name of your company). Each page is assigned a default URL consisting of numbers. Your username should be such that it reflects the topic of your page or the name of your entire company so that search engines and customers can easily find your business in Google and Facebook searches. You need at least 25 likes if you want this URL.

Use descriptive keywords in the "About" section

The About section on your Facebook page is considered the primary source of textual property you own. Make sure the description of your business and products is as accurate as possible and use keywords that users can use when searching for their questions. While selecting the keywords, ensure that you go through other Facebook pages similar to yours and pick some keywords from there. Ask yourself, if someone had to search for your business or brand online, what are the words they would likely associate with your brand? Make a list of such words and keep it handy.

You should also always include the URL of your website in the description you provide. This will encourage users to click on it.

Use the appropriate category for your business

Most often, companies and businesses tend to choose the wrong category. In this way, they reduce the likelihood of being displayed in the Facebook chat search. If you're a local business, you need to make sure you pick the right category for your business. There are different categories to choose from like celebrities, bands, artists, local business, company, organization, charity or a community, but try to pick the one that most accurately describes you and your business or brand.

Optimize the images on your page

The first thing people see when they visit your site is your cover image and profile photo. The images you use should be of good quality and reflect what your brand wants to emit. The images used must be of reasonable size. This means that the photo on the cover should be about 851 x 315 pixels in size, and the profile image should have a size of 160 x 1160 pixels. Avoid grainy or poor-quality images. The images you use must also be relevant to your brand or business and should not be random. For example, if you are a local restaurateur, then posting images about the latest developments in the automobile industry doesn't make any sense.

Pinned posts

No matter what you think, most users only visit your page once. They are interacting with your page through the news displayed in their newsfeed, but they don't usually open your business page over and over again.

For this reason, the main function of your page is to convince the user to click the Like button. Facebook allows the page administrator to attach a message to the top of the page. Make sure that the topic of this post, which can be attached, is interesting and unique and attracts the attention of the page visitor.

Use Facebook Groups

The main tool that all businesses on Facebook should use to market their business is a Facebook page. But even groups can be an effective marketing strategy in different industries and niches. When used properly, groups can help generate a lot of traffic and even increase your business engagement. By participating in other industry groups, you can establish yourself as an authority in your field. Providing useful tips and useful information will help you become a valuable member of a group, and once people trust you, they will want to learn more about you and your business.

One of the most important uses of the Facebook group may be to create and participate in groups that are within your area of interest. Groups allow you to interact personally with your audience. It will also help your company to engage in regular discussions with your target audience.

Create a group that is responsive to anything that has to do with your niche or industry. For example, if you were a contractor, it would be a good idea to set up a group on Facebook where people can ask questions or discuss repairs, construction projects, and more. You can include all other users who you think will be able to contribute to the group or might at least help with your promotional efforts.

Promote Social Sharing on Facebook

Your corporate website and Facebook need to work together. Your sales funnel, or the journey a potential customer goes on when deciding to make a purchase helps direct the traffic from your Facebook page to your blog or website.

However, you also need to make sure that you give visitors to your site the ability to like and share the pages on Facebook, as well as to interact with your site. Make sure all content on your site has a Like and Share button that appears right next to it. These buttons can be added manually, or you can use various third-party services like AddThis or even the WordPress plugin to customize your buttons and make adding them to your website easier. You can also add something like "View posts" to give your site visitors a preview of the type of content that is typically posted on your social media pages.

Increase the Visibility of Your Posts

A common complaint that the majority of site owners share is that most of their fans have not seen their posts on Facebook. Facebook successfully studied this problem, and they managed to narrow the problem down to two main factors.

The first is the amount of content published on Facebook. This means that the user's newsfeed does not have enough space to display each message. The competition for publishing and appearing in the user's newsfeed is very stiff, and this results in a reduction of the impact on regular posts.

The second reason for limiting the visibility of the post is that the Facebook algorithm has been designed to display only the content most relevant to its users. Relevance is now determined by many factors, including the way a person interacted with a page in the past, the type of posts published, and the popularity of previous posts on the page among its users. Simply put, the more popular your posts are, the more visible they are. The following two tips can improve the visibility of your posts in the fan feed.

- Using video in your publishing strategy. Videos are more attractive and can help attract the viewer's attention.

- Look at the Insights page to determine the type of content that appeals to your audience. Page Insights typically contain a lot of content-type data that can help you interact more with your audience. Find out about the formats of the messages that are most visible (images, videos, links, or lyrics) and topics that appeal to your audience. Also, keep track of the days and times, as well as the frequency of publishing, that seem to work very well with your audience.

To get the most out of your advertising, you need to make sure the content you provide is attractive. Yes, you can use Facebook to publicize your business, but this is also an opportunity to create and maintain lasting relationships with your target audience. Ask yourself, "Will my fans find this article interesting for reading and interacting, even if they are not interested in buying a product I offer?"

When and How Often to Send

Some business owners focus on publishing at the right time and on the right day to ensure optimal coverage and interaction. However, the truth is that there is no fixed approach to publishing that meets the needs of all users. Online research may be available on this topic. However, please do your research. Be sure to consult Facebook Insights to make sure these methods fit your target audience.

Some people tend to believe that posting on Thursdays and Fridays results in a higher level of participation, and others believe that posting between noon and 3:00 pm helps maximize visibility. You can test these two theories yourself with Facebook Insights.

When it comes to the frequency of publication, you need to understand that there is a difference in being informative and annoying. Spamming your page with multiple posts will discourage your audience from following you. Some companies have managed to publish 5 to 10 times a day, and some may publish 1 to 3 messages a week, and they find that this is also effective.

SocialBaker, an artificial intelligence-backed social media marketing company, has found that posting less than two posts a week does not help attract your audience, and you may even lose interaction with them. If you publish more than two posts per day, you bombard your audience with too much information. Therefore, the ideal number of posts you should publish per week should be between 5 and 10. This will help to ensure maximum engagement.

Use Paid Options

It is quite possible to use free strategies to achieve decent visibility for your messages. But you should strongly consider looking for ways to supplement these organic strategies with some paid ones.

Currently, Facebook has two ways to increase the reach of your posts. The first one is by boosting the post. That way, you can improve the visibility of your message in your user's news feed. You can choose to have your message appear to subscribers to your page, your fans' friends, or other users you select. The targeting options available to your message include your interests, age, gender, and location of your ideal audience. To improve a specific post, you must click "Boost" when creating a new post. You'll also find this option in old posts if you want to extend an already published post. Improving the quality of posts is a very simple and effective way to increase the reach of your posts.

The second way to use paid options is to promote posts. They can be accessed through the Facebook Ad Manager. To create your advertised listing, you'll need to open the Facebook Ad Creator and click on the "Enlarge" option for your posts. Even though this is called a "promotion," the targeting and budgeting parameters can be better customized than just the "promotion" option on the page.

When Should a Specific Post be Advertised?

One of the main difficulties for business owners or marketers on Facebook is to understand when to promote a post. In general, you want to promote news that helps you achieve a specific goal, such as increasing traffic to your website or promoting the sale of a particular product. Once you have chosen the position you want to advertise, consider the STIR strategy. With this strategy, you can answer specific questions before you publish a post. STIR is the acronym for a strategy known as Shelf life, Timing, Impact, and Results, which are the questions you should ask yourself when considering promoting a post. Once you analyze the content according to the specific aspects of the STIR strategy, you will be able to decide whether you must promote such content or not.

CHAPTER 6

BUILDING A BRAND USING YOUR PERSONAL PAGE

If you're still not using Facebook to make people aware of your business or brand, you're wasting a perfectly great opportunity to make use of the world's most powerful marketing platform. As mentioned earlier, using Facebook gives you the opportunity to tap a lot of prospects for your brand or business. Can you imagine how many prospects – in absolute terms – you can tap even if you just aim for less than 1% of the social media behemoth's total membership of more than 1 billion people? And consider the fact that an average mobile user spends 1 minute of every 5 on Facebook – that makes for a very rich sea of prospects! Wow!

While many entrepreneurs keep their personal and business or brand pages separate, it doesn't mean you can't use your personal page to help promote the latter page and build more awareness and business about and for your brand. Consider that because business' pages contribute a lot of revenue for Facebook, it can be quite challenging to get meaningful engagement without spending on ads. Remember the issue about increasing ad revenues competing for organic or natural reach? While they seem to be working for a great number of entrepreneurs, as indicated by increasing ad revenues, why not supplement your Facebook advertising campaigns with another potentially effective – and free – supplement, which is your personal page?

The good news is that your personal page can help your business or brand's page get more attention or awareness. The bad news – if you'll look at it that way, depending on your perspective, is that it may take a bit more effort and time. But I believe that the results can be worth it.

Here's how you can use your personal Facebook page to augment your business or brand's page:

Professionalism

If you'd like to use your personal page to supplement or augment your business or brand page, make sure that it's representative of your brand or business – it should be professional. A good and simple way of doing it is to avoid posting things that you don't want your business or brand's stakeholders – suppliers, customers, employees and prospects – to see. You wouldn't want to turn off any of your stakeholders, especially your prospects and customers.

Another good and simple guideline to help keep your page professional is to avoid posting stuff that shows you drinking, partying like hell or anything that's potentially offensive or immoral. It's very easy to lose several followers, friends and prospects with a very stupid post and very hard to win them back.

Control

To maximize your efforts in using your personal page to augment your business or brand's page, it's best for you to make all your posts visible to the public, i.e., everyone. Privacy isn't an option when it comes to posts because the goal is to reach as many people as possible for the sake of your brand or business.

But accessibility to your posts should only be limited to viewing them. You'll need to keep people from just posting on your timeline or tagging you in their posts on their own or other people's walls. Turn on the option that allows you to first approve any posts or tags on your page before being shown on your wall. That way, you can minimize or even mitigate the risk of any incriminating or integrity-eroding posts making it to your page.

Sociable

One of the best ways to win followers – and engage them enough for the benefit of your brand or business – is by often adding people as Facebook friends and approving as many real people friend requests as possible. Marketing and building brand or business awareness is a numbers game and as such, add as much Facebook friends as you can on your page. Just ensure they're real people.

Keep It Un-Politicized

While it's true that we are all free to support the politicians and political issues that we want to and express such support, it doesn't mean it's good for business. Since the goal is to promote your business or brand's page, it's best not to step on other people's toes by expressing political sentiments on your Facebook page that may offend people who may have a significantly different opinion from yours. If you really need to vent off, there are many other and healthier avenues for that like friends and other people who are as open-minded as you.

Positivity

Believe me, no one's going to be interested with your whines and rants. Worse, it may even turn off people enough to dislike your brand or business as well. Can you imagine the overflow to their mother teams if LeBron James or Cam Newton complained about how the NBA or NFL sucks (theoretically speaking only, ok?), respectively? That's what I'm talking about.

A good but simple rule of thumb here is this: if you can't say it to your date on your first meeting, don't say it on Facebook either.

Tag wisely

While tagging people you've been with at events in your posts may be considered as good technique and appropriate for increasing your posts' reach to other people's followers too, it's inappropriate to tag people in posts in which they have nothing to do with just for the sake of increasing your reach. That's unwise, unethical and annoying, all of which can backfire on your attempts to promote your brand or business.

Profile Picture

If your profile picture presents you half-naked or in a really skimpy swimsuit, replace it even if you look hot. More so if your profile picture features you in a very goofy and silly mode. It's just not professional (remember the first tip?).

However, I'm not saying that you should be in a 3-piece suit or in a business dress for your profile picture. Nah, just make it interestingly decent. Since you're representing your business or brand, your picture shouldn't give people the impression that your business is either silly or stiff. Go for profile pictures that's neither too business-y nor silly or goofy. It should represent both you and your brand well enough while generating enough interest to engage your friends or your brand's prospects.

Like Often

You can make more people more aware of your posts – and consequently your brand's page – by liking other people or brands' posts. Whenever you skip over other people's posts without "like"-ing them, you'll send Facebook the signal that you're not interested in that person or brand and over time, it'll stop showing their posts on your news feeds. And when you don't see their posts, you won't be able to like them frequently enough to make them see yours, which begins a downward spiral of posts invisibility.

More than just posts, it will also help you a lot if you like as much of other people's or brand's comments on your personal posts. You can engage more people simply by acknowledging their comments via "like". By engaging them more, you increase the chances of engaging them even more and signal to Facebook's algorithms to show their posts on your news feeds regularly.

Like often to engage often.

Birthday Greets

Another great way to engage more people is by greeting them on Facebook on their birthdays. It sends the signal that they're relatively important to you. When people feel appreciated enough, they're encouraged to act more favorably towards you – and your brand.

Postography

What I mean by this is to the extent possible, always include a photo in all your posts and don't just post using texts alone. Remember the saying that a picture paints a thousand words? As such, posts with pics tend to grab more attention from viewers and Facebook itself tends to promote posts with pictures much more than text-only ones.

And speaking of postography, always share your Instagram posts on Facebook by clicking on the "share to Facebook" button. It doubles your photographic posts exposure via dual platforms as well as increases your posts promotion by Facebook since Facebook tends to promote Instagram-shared posts more than direct photographic posts.

The Value of Timing

The faster your posts accumulate likes and comments, the more Facebook promotes your posts. And the ability of accumulating such likes and comments quickly is highly influenced by the timing of your posts.

There are times of the day – or night – where in most of your followers tend to be actively online and it can be very beneficial for you if you're able to estimate such times. Unfortunately, the only way to really know is by trial and error – observe the relationships between your posts' timing and the number of likes or comments they get to get a rough estimate.

Informatively Interesting

When it comes to engaging posts, content rules! A purely text post that says "It's freezing outside" will get way less views and engagement as compared to a post of a picture of a popsicle with clothes and shoes outside.

Posts that directly try to sell stuff is another kind of post that's sure to garner low viewership and elicit very little to no engagement and as such, must be avoided. The best way to sell – if you really need to – on Facebook is indirectly through stories or mentions. You'll have to meticulously craft your posts so that they're interesting enough to garner views and interactions or engagement to help promote and build your brand or business' page. A very good way to do this is to make use of humor and avoid being self-focused, i.e., narcissistic. Should you feel the need to post something about yourself, make it fun so people will like you and consequently, your brand or business.

CHAPTER 7

FACEBOOK ADVERTISEMENTS.

The leading blog writers are utilizing Facebook advertisements to advertise their blog site. What they do is compose a post as well as pay Facebook to advertise it to the appropriate individuals. Although they can obtain quite costly, leading blog writers utilize this approach to expand their organization each month.

The terrific aspect of Facebook advertisements is that they will certainly reveal your advertisements to individuals that have an interest in your post. Additionally, it targets individuals that are searching for what you use. You will certainly see a great deal even more conversion prices or individuals registering for your blog owner as well as acquiring your associate items, all thru Facebook advertisements instead of cost-free website traffic. Do not obtain me incorrect cost-free website traffic is still great, yet Facebook advertisements are a whole lot extra targeted than any type of various other website traffic resource available.

Currently we will not enter the entire procedure of producing Facebook advertisements, yet what I will certainly state is this once you have a consistent revenue from your blog site I desire you to spend it in advertising and marketing. It will certainly aid you take your blog site to the following degree, and also obtain you closer to the $100,000 a month mark.

Producing your item

We spoke about sophisticated web traffic, utilizing Facebook advertisements to obtain even more individuals onto your blog site. Currently we're likely to speak about utilizing your item rather than associate web links, and also associate items are terrific to make an earnings from blogging. Nonetheless, if you wish to take your revenue to the following degree from blogging, producing your item is the method to go.

Depending upon your specific niche, you can either determine to construct your training course or to offer your items. For example, individuals that remain in the particular niche of exactly how to generate income on-line develop programs on just how to earn money online. The most effective component concerning training courses is that you can bill upwards to $1,000 an item to educate a person just how to earn money online and also individuals will certainly pay you.

So if you have 500,000 energetic visitors to your blog site as well as just 1% of these individuals get your program at $1,000, that is close to 5 million bucks in profits. The bright side regarding this technique is that you reach maintain all of it. Every blog owner that is making 100,000 a month will certainly need to either begin offering goods of their brand name or they will certainly need to make program addressing an issue.

One point to bear in mind, individuals are most likely to get if they have a trouble which is immediate for many viewers. As an example, exactly how to generate income or exactly how to shed body fat is an outstanding instance of resolving an issue. If your blog site is pastime relevant such as vehicles or taking a trip after that I would certainly suggest you stick in the direction of offering goods.

Training

This technique is just pertaining to specific niches which aid address an issue. So if you enjoy physical fitness specific niche or just how to generate income online specific niche, this would certainly be a wonderful endeavor to participate on. When you have actually developed on your own as an experienced individual in your particular niche, what you can begin doing is billing individuals for on the internet training.

For example, if you remain in the physical fitness particular niche, you can make an on the internet tailored training strategy. For individuals that remain in the exactly how to generate income specific niche, they can have training require sale. Individuals are spending for on the internet training as well as much like programs, you can bill a great deal of cash.

Individuals are billing $500 a hr of Skype telephone call. It is adept when it concerns getting to $100,000 a month earnings. See to it you are considering this technique in order to expand your blog site right into the 6 number a month revenue resource you have actually been desiring.

There are a great deal of service concepts as well as endeavors you can require to expand your blog site right into a six-figure a month blog site. Nevertheless, these are the main approaches individuals are making use of to reach that six-figure a month revenue.

Lots of Facebook marketers are utilizing these techniques effectively to make 7 numbers a year. As soon as you have actually accomplished your objective of making 3k a month reread this phase. Like I discussed initially, this phase is to obtain your juices moving and also to reveal you just how to scale your service up also additionally. Keeping that note, we pertain to an end of this phase.

CHAPTER 8

TYPES OF FACEBOOK ADS

If you are among the one billion brands on Facebook, you might have noticed the changing trend when it comes to content. Video materials are taking over the newsfeed and proving to be one of the greatest content types of 2019.

As a social media marketer, you should understand the importance of videos for your brand. There are different types of video format available for brands. Each Facebook video ad type allow the businesses to showcase their best products. The marketing specialists on the platform are becoming aware of this rising trend, too, and trying to adopt various styles. As an entrepreneur, therefore, you want to focus on brand awareness and sales growth.

Previous statistics show that static images or text-based posts do not bring as much engagement as videos lately. In 2018, a research conducted by Adobe Digital Insights found that a lot of advertisers lose sales and audiences when they try the one-size-fits-all method in the United States. There are diverse types of Facebook ads that you can adopt to run your campaigns as well. However, there is no definite rule that says that you should only use a single ad type. Brands can try different materials to see which one brings in the most engagement.

Nevertheless, everything drops down to the fact that you have to stand out among everyone. How can you compete with your competitors on Facebook advertisements while maintaining the quality standards and customers' interest? To accomplish this, you first need to understand different types of Facebook ads. Once you are well-versed with their importance, you can test them to engage with users on your page.

Showstopper - Video Ads

As discussed earlier, Facebook video ads are the top forms of advertisements that a brand can adopt. Videos are indeed a showstopper when it comes to user engagement and brand awareness. Instead of spending your time on writing short chunks of text or uploading a picture on your page, you can work on an engaging video either in-house or by hiring a professional videographer. Alternatively, you can upload your own native videos as long as they are of high quality. If you are filling your videos with useless content and fillers, then chances are that you will not get any views on it. The first 10 seconds of your video should convey the message of what users can expect to see later. Punch lines that attracts the customers' attention are going to work well on videos, too.

Consider the example of Nike's new ad - "Nike – Dream Crazier" - this year. It lasted for only a minute and 30 seconds, but it managed to grasp the interest of viewers because of its title, content, as well as emotions conveyed through it. It was well-strategized as Nike released it with the message, "Show them what crazy dreams seem like." It positively provoked the feelings of viewers around the globe and became a perfect representation of an impactful video. Instead of focusing on your brand's great points, therefore, you should incorporate human emotions into your advertisements to create a sense of relatability.

Why Invest in Video Ads?

Video ads are the best form of Facebook advertisements as they ensure that people will remember your business. Visually appealing ads help you shine brighter than your competitors. They also work well for converting viewers into customers. Furthermore, ads provide enough data to marketers, which they can utilize on other platforms such as Instagram, Twitter, and LinkedIn.

Research shows that video content advertisements are going to stay for long and will allow brands to communicate with their audiences in a more interactive way. A survey conducted by Hubspot earlier in 2019 also indicated that videos aren't just effective; instead, they are becoming a necessity for the brands. Some of the marketing facts and statistics to support the importance of video ads are shown below.

- Approximately 54% of the population on social media platforms want to see video content rather than static images or text-based posts.

- The region that most demands for video content is Latin America.

- Approximately 83% of the users across the web watch YouTube videos. This information indicates that clips available on any platform are going to attract more viewership and engagement than other visual types. Thus, it creates an opportunity for brands to share their content or story through videos and run ads using them to reach potentials users.

- There can be different video genres that can be adopted by brands. However, adopting to an entertaining type of videos generate more engagement. Around 73% of the population shows interest in "entertaining" videos as well, and so businesses should add elements of entertainment relevant to their products or services.

Before starting your own video-based campaigns on Facebook, you need to define a clear message that you want to convey through that visual type. You also have to decide about the ultimate objective of your advertisement. Say, do you want to send people from your video to a particular landing page, reach more potential clients within your locality, or something else? Nevertheless, when it comes to video ads, brands usually select "Get Video Views" with an aim to achieve potential leads from it.

Workable Video Marketing Strategies to Increase User Engagement, Conversions, and Overall Play Rate

Videos with No Sound

This may sound absurd, but videos with no sound can actually attract consumers' attention. In this rapidly evolving social world, people don't have time to go through details and prefer to swipe through their newsfeed instead. Videos with sound may restrict them from open them, though, in certain scenarios.

To convey your message through a video without using sound, you can add subtitles to it. This will help viewers know what's going on in your video. Facebook recently shared a caption feature for advertisers considering the sound issue. Now, you may promote ads on mute. As a marketer or advertiser, it is important to invest in videos that sell while maintaining the factors of creativity and useful information.

Turn On Autoplay Feature

Would you want your Facebook video to get noticed? Users don't have the time to wait as they merely spend few seconds to see what a brand has to offer. If your video isn't on autoplay, chances are that you are going to lose potential views and clicks. So, if you want to engage those multitaskers, you need to ensure that your videos will play automatically. However, to become eligible to set videos on Autoplay, your brand has to bid for cost per impression (CPM) on Facebook. Cost per click (CPC) isn't going to help here because you need to get impressions, not clicks.

Keep It Short

Video ads are supposed to be short. Facebook allows a user to upload a two-hour long video, but who has the time to see an advertisement like that? If you want to gain attention, you need to focus on what they want to see and deliver it in the initial 45 seconds of the video.

In 2016, Wistia released data about how users engage with videos and how much time they spend on average. The data showed that, on average, around 80% of individuals watch videos that are shorter than 30 seconds. People lose interest if the video gets longer than that, and they usually drop out after 30 seconds. If you want to stay in a safe zone, you can try to keep your video duration within the time limit of two minutes.

Fun Fact: Your 90-second video is going to leave the same impact as your 30-second video on the viewers. Just keep its duration under two minutes, and you are good to go.

Only Promote Videos That Performed Well on Other Platforms

To determine which videos performed well, you would have to ask yourself a few questions. For instance, which ones performed organically on your page? What kind of content was used in those videos that generated the most views? Which one among the live or recorded webinars gained most user engagement? It is important to realize the status of these core components - e.g., engagement, views, and shares of the previous videos - so that you can run similar video ads in the future. Investing money on them will help you gain more viewership, sales and user engagement.

Focus on Targeted Audience

Focused ads can bring potential leads and increase your sales. Instead of capitalizing on a video ad campaign that targets a vague and larger audience, it is better to granulize your target market and concentrate on people who are genuinely interested in the type of products or services you are offering. This way, you have great chances of receiving high engagement rate on your videos. This will also help in converting your viewers into potential customers. You can run ads using targeted audience, specific locations, demographics, interests, and behaviors of the users. Social media marketers can apply this strategy on different focus groups to see which ones bring in the best results.

Image-Based Advertisements

At first, Facebook advertising seems easy to set up and run. In reality, it's a bit tricky. Nevertheless, the more time you invest into planning your campaign, the more traffic it can bring to your content.

Although video ads got their place in the advertisement marathon, there is one great ad type that we cannot neglect when it comes to visually appealing content: image-based advertisements. The truth is that Facebook offered "picture advertisements" as one of its initial marketing tools. To bring the right traffic on your content, social media marketers need to adjust all the important aspects of it into one visually and aesthetically enticing image ad.

Image-based advertisements are one of the top ad types on Facebook. To successfully run this material, you should keep track of some of the technical requirements to ensure that the advertisement starts off with a bang. While the picture ads are the most basic ones, they are the most effective options as well. They are versatile in nature and can be used for any brand goal, e.g., brand awareness, sales or user engagement. Social Media Marketers can keep track of the following aspects:

- The image size should be no smaller than 1200 x 638 pixels. Any photo with dimensions lower than that will become distorted and may not be accepted by Facebook.

- Consider the platform's 20% rule. This means that you can only add 90 characters of text. If you will add too many words on the picture, Facebook may not run it even if you set a high budget. The site introduced this rule back in 2018, which has brought a lot restrictions for the advertisers. It has become important for brands to keep minimum text on the images to run them properly on Facebook. This rule only applies on newsfeed advertisements, though, and not on right-panel advertisements.

Pro tip: Make sure to check your images on a 20% rule checker online to see where they stand in terms of text overlay. If every photo gets marks "OK," you are good to go.

Image ads are one of the great materials to showcase your products to potential customers and create awareness about them. Marketers need to understand that visually appealing pictures don't need to be difficult or expensive. A simple and elegant picture with an impactful text can bring in the right audience to your brand.

Image ads run directly in the newsfeed of the users. Brands get the ultimate chance to present their products to the world through a vibrant and impactful image. Marketers can use images of actual items in the ads to represent what the business is all about and what users can expect if they buy a particular product.

Another important aspect to keep in mind is the involvement of real humans into the ad. For instance, if you sell funky socks, you can either take an unappealing picture and post with a text or have models photographed while wearing those socks for your ad campaigns. Ads that show a familiar sense of social fabric for users generate more engagement and sales than those with only a product image.

Excessive text on ads can distract the audience and can result in less user engagement. Research shows that images with no to minimum text leave a more positive impact on consumers as compared to those cluttered with too much text. So, as a marketer, you need to keep track of this point for future image-based advertisements. The rule of thumb is to keep one message per image ad campaign. For example, if you are promoting a certain product or the upcoming launch of a new line, you have to make sure that each ad delivers a single message. It is vital to keep the ultimate goal in mind while downsizing the point of focus across your campaigns using different ad sets.

Furthermore, think about the visual consistency of the ad campaign. If you are running an ad campaign for a particular product, ensure that the color themes, font types, et cetera are consistent throughout the advertisement. Together, they will be able to deliver one message and help you run the brand's ads in a successful manner.

Users on Facebook prefer to see quality content, and that is where the marketers come in. It is your responsibility to use high-resolution images for the advertisements, for one. This will help you to promote ads on Facebook and adhere to the platform's quality standards at once.

Your brand doesn't have to hire a professional photographer to create appealing images. All you need to do is to pay attention to a few important aspects, such as the size and quality of the images that you plan to use in your advertisements.

Lastly, for the static picture ads marketers can experiment with different type of visuals to see what works best for a particular brand.

Collection Advertisements - E-Commerce Gateway

As discussed above, there are different Facebook ad types that brands can choose to promote their content with. However, some ads perform better than others, especially if you apply certain hacks and tricks. Talking about a great performing material, Facebook collection ads work like a charm if used correctly. This type of advertisement has a solid background of success stories. Considering you want your brand to be the next success story, you should incorporate collection ads into your brand's marketing strategies.

Collection ads were introduced back in 2017 and managed to grab the attention of advertisers due to their impressive performance, convenient design, and flexible customization options. A usual collection ad includes either a video or an image followed by relevant product pictures. This ad type is great for brands that want to show several goods to the users without making the advertisement overwhelming for them.

One of the recent success stories showed that, during Christmas in 2018, Sephora ran a couple of ads using Facebook's collection ad format and received a 32% increase on their return on investment (ROI). This is an example for all the brands out there that they can test and run a collection ad format for their own products and services.

When users click on your collection ads, they are redirected to a new window where a full image of the product gets displayed. Not only does it enhance the user engagement, but it also boosts sales. Most of the users prefer to scroll through their newsfeed using a mobile device; thus, it is important for marketers to optimize their ads accordingly. The great news is that collection ads work great on smartphones and tablets as they are specifically designed for mobile ads only and to maximize the experience of mobile users.

Facebook is now all about advertisement and how you use different tools to develop your brand awareness. They are best suited for users who are always looking for something new to look for. Customize your collection ads in a way that each one delivers the message of your ultimate campaign and ultimately converts your ad visitors into buyers.

Collection ads make a win-win situation for both marketers and Facebook as well, considering high-quality ads bring user engagement to the posts even from those individuals who are not very active on maintaining their profiles. There is a pool of people who do not use Facebook for connections. They keep it for shopping purposes since Facebook is becoming more of a business medium for both brands and individual consumers. A simple yet interactive video coupled with product images can attract the right audience and will increase the engagement rate on both the posts and the Facebook page.

Facebook collection ads are one of the core boosters for e-commerce market. If you run a brand that works in an e-commerce sector, and you still haven't added the collection ads in your marketing campaigns, then you are missing out on a lot of things. Collection ads are dynamic forms of advertisement that represent the actual brand identity along with products in front of potential users. You should invest into this particular ad type because collection ads help not only in selling goods but also in promoting your store with an extra flair and building your brand's image.

There are standard templates offered under the umbrella of collection ads, including: Instant Storefront, Instant Lookbook, Instant Storytelling, and Instant Customer Interest and Acquisition. These templates come in handy when creating interactive and vibrant advertising tools. Marketers always have the option to customize the ads as per brand owner's preferences and campaign objectives. Yo can see which ad sets are working and which aren't as well by trying different styles. The A/B testing provides a great platform to marketers to set different details for the same product. The core components to keep in focus are:

- Headlines for each ad

- Offers proposed on both ads

- Copywriting done for each ad

- Visuals used on the main cover image of the advertisement

- Type and quality of product images used on both ad sets

All of these elements will help marketers see the performance of each ad and find out what factors influenced the sales through their campaigns.

Carousel Advertisements

Facebook carousel advertisements are among the most engaging and interactive ad types that brands can utilize to sell their products. Carousel ads are popular not merely because they are effective for the user engagement but also because of their layout options. After all, they provide a clean and concise medium to present the product line of a brand and allow a more interactive way of storytelling. These types of ads are a huge hit among e-commerce businesses as well. So, anyone who wants to sell their goods in a creative manner can invest into carousel advertisements.

Now, you will notice that most of the advertisers use the play cards to promote different aspects of one product. Social media marketers can use up to ten images to create a carousel ad. This means that you will have the leverage to promote ten different products under the umbrella of one ad. Carousel ads usually consist of ten cards, and each one can showcase what your brand has to offer. The latter has a separate description underneath every image, too, to explain the story behind that the product. This feature makes it super efficient for the brands as it allows the marketers to add different call-t0-action buttons under each merchandise and lead to their specific landing pages. This is the amazing ad flexibility that you don't get with any other ad type. With the opportunity to use ten cards, you can target your potential prospects and let them know what you have to offer. One statistic indicates that carousel ads cost relatively less -

approximately 30% to 50% in cost-per-conversions and approximately 20% to 30% in cost-per-click - as compared to a standard image-based advertisement.

Carousel ads work best for the desktop placements. This ad type comes with a series of different cards; that's why businesses can demonstrate their story in a more elaborate way. Just because most users use mobile for internet browsing, though, the importance of desktop ads can be neglected by the brands already. A majority of Facebook users still prefer to use desktop when viewing their account on the platform. You might not receive the same amount of user engagement as with collection ads, but using carousel ads can shed light to your brand and create an impactful image in users' mind and help you see an increase in the sales of promoted products.

There are other prominent perks of using carousel ads that brands can adopt for their own benefit and success as marketers can include them to their social media marketing strategy. One of the most important benefits that you can gain from carousel ads is the fact that it can be placed on both desktop and mobile. This option is not available for collection ads since they work on mobile placements only.

One advantage that carousel ads can also offer is the ease of ad customization and creation. This gives the marketers an opportunity to make the advertisements more personal and drive traffic to specific landing pages through each carousel card. To evoke user interest in your products make, sure to play around with the designs, make interactive slideshows or use a mix of videos and pictures to portray your brand's message creatively. You can choose a total of four images (it can be one video that's supported by three images, for instance) in the main preview section. Make sure to use the top four contents in your preview ad, though, to attract users' attention for other carousel cards within the same advertisement.

Best Practices for Carousel Ads

Carousel ads are easy to set up and do not take much time to get customized and placed in comparison with collection ads. However, social media marketers can use some of the best practices below to make their ads look more creative and professional.

Always Use a CTA

The inclusion of CTAs can improve user engagement and click-through rate on your ads. If you are not getting audience, the budget that your brand has invested in the advertisement will practically go to waste.

Use Numerous Headlines

As a social media marketer it is your responsibility to test and try different headlines on each carousel card. This will help you understand which carousel card brought in the most traffic and which didn't. Then, on the basis of the results, you can use similar content and design type on future ads. This method can work well for various brands since you can highlight numerous offers or prominent features on each card.

Tell Your Brand's Story through a Series of Cards

If you are using enticing graphics and content in your carousel cards, then chances are that you will attract more traffic from people who want to learn more about your offers. It is indeed an amazing tactic to bring in the new potential customers to your landing pages either on Facebook or business website.

Instant Experience Advertisements

Considering the proliferation of Facebook advertisements and their types, there are still some unexplored techniques that marketers can use to boost sales and brand awareness. However, only few take the charge of exploring. So, if you want to stand out among your competitors, you should read along to learn about one of the unexplored gems of Facebook advertisements: Instant Experience.

Exploration and usage of innovative techniques tend to perform well and bypass the generic ad perceptions and techniques that are blindly followed by the Facebook page admins or marketers. To understand the mechanism of what works on Facebook, marketers need to invest extra time to understand the changing Facebook algorithms and newsfeed. Once you get hold of what works through tried innovative techniques, you can start using those methods that bring your brand in the spotlight.

Instant Experience advertisements are one of those techniques that you must consider to bring an extra charm to your brand. Instant Experiment ads were formally known as "canvas ads" when they first rolled out. However, the name changed after a while based on different components, such as how instantly users reacted to the ads, what the reactions on the ads were, and so on. Instant Experience ads enable a business to showcase a compelling brand history and story outside the confined walls of a regular feed. Facebook users can learn about the business by staying on its page and not getting redirected to external links, e.g., a website. This allows the social media advertiser to create an enthralling experience for the users by providing the type of content that they want to see. A comfortable browsing experience, after all, is one of the important aspects to look upon in Facebook advertisements, regardless of the ad type selected. Moving on, the platform encourages and promotes instant ads happily, considering the users don't get to leave Facebook.

Pro Hack: Facebook favors and appreciates instant experience advertisements over the regular traditional ones.

However, most social media marketers avoid using Instant Experience advertisements, which is a big loss for companies and leaves a lot of opportunities behind. The major reasons behind this decision are rooted to the fact that these ads require more time and attention to details than traditional ads, they seem more complicated in terms of settings and customization, and they require more creativity to hook the right audience. If you are among those brands, then you should reconsider utilizing this form of advertisement. Instant Experience ads are the breakthrough type of advertisement that can genuinely introduce a lot of potential clients to your products. So, if you want to take advantage of this amazing Facebook ad type, then invest in your time in creating visually appealing designs and support them with relatable headlines. Even if you don't have pro designing skills, you can always use pre-made Facebook templates, which have been designed specifically for Instant Experience ads.

- See some of the major advantages of using this marketing tool below.

- They are light-weighted ads and load instantly.

- They are properly optimized for the mobile users and perform well on the same medium.

- They are designed and formatted in a way that attracts the attention of the users, especially the targeted audience, and that is beneficial to the brand.

- It allow consumers to interact with brands, engage in interactive conversations, swipe through images and videos, as well as pan and tilt the advertisements to explore new products.

- It provides pre-made versatile Facebook ad templates that marketers without professional designing abilities can use.

- Instant Experience Ads can be expanded on a full screen to improve users' buying experience.

- They are designed to work on all formats, including static images, videos, graphics, slideshows, carousel, and even on collection ads.

Brands can utilize this innovative approach towards advertising to ensure user involvement and brand awareness. It's a great way to showcase what a brand has to offer to potential and existing customers. As a marketer, you will need some time to adopt the working mechanism of Instant Experience ads. However, once you get accustomed to it, you can definitely see the obvious changes that it will bring to the table. To start successfully, make sure to use your own premium product images along with unique content to be able to compete against the mainstream ads on Facebook. Make sure to use a simple and easy-to-follow pathway for the users as well using CTAs, texts, links, and buttons that can enhance users' buying experience.

Facebook is a great platform when it comes to promoting your products and services. Overtime, it has developed into a great medium for both brands and customers. Considering the amazing details that Instant Experience advertisements provide, marketers now have more control over what they want to show and sell to their users. Similarly, from the users' perspective, they can explore different buying options at a single space and invest their money on the desired products or services that they appreciate. Even if you are only starting as a new brand, investing into instant ads can boost your brand's presence and create a positive image for your goods. You don't have to set aside a large amount of dollars these ads; use a limited budget that suits your brand and keep your focus on the quality of graphics and headlines.

CHAPTER 9

HOW TO DEVELOP A FACEBOOK LIKE CAMPAIGN

Once you create a page, your thoughts are probably revolving around getting likes since this is a mark of how large your audience is. Creating a page is easy; gaining likes is the hard part. Going from your first like to 100 then 500 to infinity is hard. Here, I will provide you with easy to implement ideas to increase your page likes. Let us jump right in

Page tagging

Facebook tagging system is the most amazing way to attract likes and visitors to your page. How do you tag? Easy, all to have to do is post about your page on your personal Facebook profile. You can use @yourfacebookpage to create awareness about your page since your posts appear in your friends' newsfeeds. The trick to this is to use creativity to coin a message that gets the attention of your Facebook friends. This is especially useful for any business that intends to run some sort of special promotion or useful content.

Suggest the page to friends

Do you remember that page orientation we did earlier on? Here is where you use it. On the side bar of your page is "suggest to friends" (see figure 4). This forms a great way to share your page with friends who are almost sure to click the like button (they are your friends after all).The trick is not overusing or abusing this option because most of your friends will get annoyed if you do.

Giveaways, promotions and contests

Let me tell you a well-guarded secret. Contents and giveaways always tick the correct boxes. Who does not love a giveaway or free merchandize? If you have a giveaway, you request those who want to participate to first like the page in order to qualify; keep in mind that Facebook no longer allows like gating (use of apps to bar people from accessing content before they can like it). A good way around this is to let your target audience know that you run random contents, promotions and giveaways hence the need for them to like your page if they are to get these. Most people will definitely not even think before clicking the like button; we all like free stuff!

Do not overlook twitter integration

Twitter for business is gaining popularity. Therefore, you can leverage this by linking your page to your company's Twitter account and converting your followers into Facebook fans.

Also, you should integrate your Facebook page with other social media sites like Pinterest, LinkedIn and Google+. This will make you leverage on the power of cross promotion making it easy for you to have a solid social media presence.

Please note that any posts you make on Facebook will also appear on your Twitter profile with a link.

CHAPTER 10

HOW TO BUILD AN EMAIL LIST

In this section, we will discuss how to construct an email list for your Facebook tries. In the event that you converse with any fruitful Facebook promoter, they will disclose to you the significance of having an email list. Having somebody's email will enable you to get in touch with them decisively. It is more probable for individuals to see and tap on your email than it is for them to get some answers concerning your most recent post online which implies you can't disregard the intensity of email and email showcasing.

I will show you today how to gather messages through free traffic and pop-ups. Gathering email can be a tedious and a relentless procedure, however significant.

I will do my best to make it basic for you. Keep in mind that building a decent email rundown will require some investment. Likewise, on the grounds that you have figured out how to gather 10,000 messages doesn't mean every one of them will tap on your email.

You have to ensure you are keeping your messages supporters connected with and sitting tight for the following email, which we will show you in this section. Finally, we will additionally manage you on the best way to make the absolute most stunning messages. It will assist you with getting a higher snap through rate. Despite the fact that email showcasing is superb, just 30% of individuals will peruse and click your email. We need to ensure we leave no stones unturned to do that and we need an elegantly composed email.

Gathering email

Toward the start of your blogging venture, you won't have a lot of cash to spend on promoting. In this part we will keep everything free assets, which means, you won't need to pay a dime on gathering any messages. Presently there are two primary ways for you to get messages. The first is through a spring up.

You can utilize email assets like MailChimp to make a free spring up. What spring up will assist you with is the point at which somebody visits your site, they will get a major box directly before them. It will approach them to agree to accept our email list so they could get a free book or something along that line, as we discussed in the past section. Contingent upon your specialty give your perusers something of significant worth.

In case you're in the wellness Niche, you can offer your perusers free eBooks on the most proficient method to put on muscle. Make sense of the considerable number of requirements and issues individuals have in your specialty. Make a free eBook or a cheat sheet and offer them for nothing. It is an absolute necessity have on your site. Odds are if individuals are on your site as of now, they won't delay to put their email in pop-ups with the expectation of complimentary data.

Presentation page

Presently the second method to gather messages is use something many refer to as a greeting page. When you join with mailchimp.com. which is allowed to utilize, you would then be able to begin making free presentation pages for your site. What greeting page will do is help you gather messages through YouTube and different destinations. In the past section, we discussed gathering messages through YouTube. This is the place greeting pages come in.

Make your presentation page through mailchimp.com. At that point duplicate that connection and post it on your YouTube recordings and different sites on the web. Your presentation page will offer a blessing in return for their email. So in the event that you go on to wellness structures and specialty sites you can gradually include your point of arrival there to explicit individuals who are into your specialty. It is likewise a superb route for you to gather messages on your YouTube recordings and other specialty related sites. You need your greeting page there fully operational. On the off chance that not, at that point you are passing up a ton of free leads.

Making email

At last, the fun part, how to make an email and how regularly you ought to send messages to your perusers. So the main thing you have to ensure is that you have your appreciated email computerized. In case you're utilizing the administrations, we prescribe mailchimp.com. You ought to have no issue robotizing email since it is extremely direct.

At whatever point somebody agrees to accept your email list, the principal thing you have to do is ensure you are sending them the blessing you have guaranteed. Your "appreciated" email will be the main mechanized email, ensure your "appreciated" email is sent following they enter their email. This would be your robotized email, since you have made you're free to email and computerized it, we will presently discuss the recurrence and the kinds of email you ought to send your endorsers.

As to rate, you ought to never email your perusers multiple times each week. There are two purposes behind it. Initially, you will have a lower shot of winding up in their spam email. Second, your perusers won't get irritated by your messages. Subsequently, they won't withdraw.

As to messages, update them about the most recent blog and the associate items you need to offer them two times every week. This is a decent principle guideline I like to live by. Not exclusively will they be locked in on the information you give them, however they will probably turn into your clients. It won't resemble you're shelled with deals pitch constantly. In the wake of attempting this for quite a long time and years, I can reveal to you this is the best strategy for messaging your perusers.

In the event that you need to have a fruitful blog, you need your perusers connected with through email. You can lose web based life following, yet the messages will live on until the end of time. Some should seriously mull over email medieval, yet most organizations are running exclusively on email showcasing. Try not to disparage the intensity of email showcasing, particularly for Facebook. Utilize these strategies we just discussed in this part to gather messages. Try not to leave any stones unturned in the event that you need to make progress in Facebook promotions.

CHAPTER 11

FACEBOOK ADS

Facebook offers various advertising options. You can choose the ad type based on different goals. As mentioned earlier, one of these goals may be to increase or promote a particular item. However, there are several options, such as promoting your page, sending others to your website, increasing conversion rates, and requesting offers from users.

After selecting your campaign goal, you can select the targeting and budgeting options and select the ad you want to use for your ad. Choosing a destination for your campaign will help you achieve your advertising goals. There are three options: a newsfeed on the desktop, a mobile newsfeed, and a column on the right. The default option is that all these options are selected. You can select the placement of the ad according to your preferences.

Spending a lot of time and money on advertising on Facebook is a pretty easy way to achieve goals, and advertising is an effective way to get traffic, likes, and conversions. However, certain practices are very effective and can help you achieve your goals in a relatively simple way.

Always use audience targeting

Advertising for a broad audience without any orientation is a tedious task, and you are preparing for failure. Not only that, but it will also be a waste of time and money because you are not guaranteed to be successful or to appeal to a large number of people. There are many options for targeting, and one thing you should try is choosing the target audience based on their behavior.

The most important content should be placed first

Most users will probably only look at the content that was placed at the beginning of your ad. For this reason, it is very important that the content that you consider important is at the very top of your ad. This can be a link or a call to action.

Rotation of advertising

If you use specific targeting for your ad and, therefore, need to serve ads to a small audience repeatedly, this means that you must change the image used for your ad every one or two weeks. Reusing the same content will simply bore your customers, and it also reduces the chances of them following your page. It is very likely that your target audience will miss your ad.

Use conversion pixels to track the performance of your ads

If you want to buy multiple ads, you should use conversion pixels to identify ads that can help you reach your goals. Facebook Pixels helps you track conversion data. You can choose from a variety of conversion types when creating a pixel. This includes checks, registrations, generated page views, leads, etc. See the Facebook Help page for more information.

Use different ads for different placements

On Facebook, you can use the same images and copy them for different ads. It is very important that created ads are created for different platforms. The announcements displayed in the newsfeed on the phone, the desktop, and the right-hand column of the desktop differ significantly. These differences should be taken into account. The ads you create for a mobile app might not be optimized for viewing on the desktop and vice versa. So, while creating ads, please ensure they are optimized for different devices.

You can also use a call-to-action to specifically tell your users what you want them to do. This encourages the users to take the action you want them to. Facebook is an excellent platform to not only find your audience but also to interact with them. When used properly, you can increase traffic flow, visibility, and conversion rate.

CHAPTER 12

HOW TO GET THE MOST OUT OF YOUR FACEBOOK LIVE

If this is your first time starting out on Facebook marketing and you're intimidated by the prospect of going Live because you never know what might happen, don't worry, you'll eventually get the hang of it. Like everything else, there's going to be a bit of a learning curve and process to it all, but you'll get more accustomed to it the more you do it.

Here are a couple of useful strategies you could keep up your sleeve to help you get the most out of your Facebook Live efforts:

- Pick Something Your Audience Is Interested In: As with everything else on social media, it is always all about the audience. For a business, nothing else matters. When planning to go Live, pick a topic of interest that your audience is sure to be interested in. For example, an upcoming product launch that you've been teasing about on Facebook in the past several weeks. You could do a live reveal of the grand unveiling and then follow that a few days later with several live segments where you break down the various tips, tricks and suggestions to help your customers get the most out of the products they've just purchased.

- Answer Their Questions: What are some of the most frequently asked questions that have been popping up across your Facebook comments? Or even through direct messages? It's a great idea to conduct a Live session to help address some of these common questions because you'll be responding to a need that your audience has. They'll be more receptive and engaged with your brand if they feel like they are being heard. You could even invite your audience to jump in and join you on the Live stream as it is happening to bring up any questions or queries they may have. This gives your content a much more authentic feel which will resonate well.

- When In the Office, Have a Studio: While Live is great for featuring on the spot moments as they happen, there will be times when you're broadcasting Live from the comfort of your own office space. When you are, it is a good idea to set up a little broadcasting studio of some sort where you can regularly host your Live sessions. This studio should be equipped with the right lighting for the best video quality, and if you have natural window light streaming into your office space, that's even better. Set up a creative little space that looks great on camera, something cozy, comfortable, and inviting. This will help you relax and feel comfortable too, as well as look aesthetically appealing to your audience.

- Involve Your Audience As Much As Possible: Mention names and give shout-outs during your Live stream broadcast. This is one of the easiest moves you could make to let your audience know they are appreciated. Remind them how much they matter to your business and help cultivate that community feel by responding to questions left in the comments, even after the Live stream has come to an end.

If you're still struggling to come up with great ideas for a Live topic, try AnswerThePublic.com, a great tool for inspiration because it lists some of the top questions which have been asked by Google. Simply narrow down the search to your related area and take a look at the questions that pop up. You could find inspiration for your next several Live videos with just a few simple clicks.

Best Practices for Your Facebook Live Content

Anything that is new can be daunting in the beginning, but don't worry, because in no time at all, you'll reach a point where broadcasting Live on Facebook is easy breezy. Being in business is a challenging endeavor for any entrepreneur, and the world of Facebook is part of that overall excitement. To help you ace your Live sessions, these best practice tips will certainly come in handy:

- Promoting Beforehand: To ensure that as many people as possible will be tuning into your Live segments, it is a good idea to try and promote the upcoming sessions before you attempt to go live. Keep them updated about when it's going to take place by updating your Facebook status with the time, date, location, and even a sneak peek into what's going to take place during the Live session. This lets your audience keep tabs on your progress so they'll be sure not to miss it.

- Strong Internet Connection Is a Must: Always check that the force is strong with your internet connection before going Live. If you're on Wi-Fi, make sure you've got great signal on your mobile device. If you're not on Wi-Fi, then you absolutely need a 4G connection for the best Live video quality possible. If your signal is too weak, you won't be able to go Live because Facebook themselves will gray out the button that says "Go Live" and you won't be able to do anything until your signal has improved.

- Go Live Where the Light Is: If you're not in your studio, go on the hunt for a location that is going to have the best lighting, and if possible, free from too much background noise and disruption. Understandably, the latter may not always be possible, especially if you're at an event or function. Whenever possible though, good lighting and minimal background noise certainly helps. Also, ensure that your camera is in the best possible position to capture the full shot of what's taking place. Cropped Live videos are a big no-no.

- Descriptions with Clarity: Always have crystal clear details included in your video. Answer the who, where, when, what, why, and how questions with every Live video description and just like that, the likelihood that your audience will click to watch your videos will increase tenfold.

- Right From Your Newsfeed: Did you know that you can actually go Live right from your Facebook newsfeed? By simply tapping on the "What's On Your Mind" section at the very top of your profile, type in a catchy description, choose your selected target audience and you're ready to go in three seconds. Easy!

- **Don't Forget Your Context:** A Live video must always have some context to it. Your audience needs to know what they're watching so they're not left confused at the end of the video wondering what that was all about. Introduce yourself at the start of the video, and give your audience a breakdown of what's taking place during this Live segment so they know what they are tuning in to watch. Let them know that you will be taking questions during the Live broadcast and encourage them to leave their questions in the comments so you can address them during this session. While waiting for your audience to jump in and type out their questions, remind them throughout the broadcast about what this session is going to cover and keep encouraging them to send their questions in. This way, those who join your Live stream later will still be caught up about what's taking place.

The biggest advantage that marketers get with this Live feature is the ability to provide the audience with an experience that is very visceral. This only increases the engagement and the interactive experience that you get to build with your audience. Be authentic and be yourself, that's probably the best approach that you could take. Don't worry about making it completely perfect, but focus instead on creating an enjoyable experience that both you and your audience will walk away from with positive feelings.

CHAPTER 13

FACEBOOK STORIES

Facebook Stories

If you want to share your adventures with all your friends and followers on Facebook, you need to use Facebook Stories. This is better than downloading a picture because it offers several options for playing the photos or videos you want to share. It's important that your advertising campaign keeps pace with the latest updates and features on Facebook.

The stories on Facebook are very similar to the news feed, but one difference between the two is that the first one is more visual. The user can add various filters and effects to the camera and publish them in the Stories section instead of downloading them as normal messages. Stories you create on Facebook can be shared with a group of people or even a single user. Once the story is published, it will be available within 24 hours and then disappear. This is very similar to Snapchat Stories.

To prepare your photos for Facebook stories, you have three options. Open the Facebook app on your mobile phone, tap the "Your Story" icon, and then tap the "Camera" icon at the top left of the screen. Then you need to press the record button to take a photo or video. If you want to share an existing photo, you can download it from the camera.

If you want to use this feature on your desktop, you will need to create a message for each publication in the news feed as usual. Once it's done, you'll need to add it to your story instead of downloading it as a regular post.

Facebook introduced the Facebook Story feature in 2017. If you want your brand or business to feel fashionable and cool, you need to be aware of any new developments that they represent.

Facebook Business Practice History

Facebook Story is a clone of Snapchat Stories or Instagram Stories. You must ensure that you are familiar with this practice before using it on your corporate site. The first thing you need to do is check before using, examine all the buttons and their functions, and then do a quick test drive.

As a business owner, you are a representative of your business, and your Facebook ad should reflect the same. This applies to not only your news but also your stories. You must make sure that the emojis, filters, colors, borders, text colors, and hashtags you use are brand oriented. Try to demonstrate your brand voice in a fun and creative way.

You must regularly and frequently publish stories on Facebook. With Facebook stories, you can quickly take a look at everything that happens to you and your business. If you want to provide your subscribers and friends with exciting updates, choose Facebook Stories. You should consider the time at which most of your subscribers will be online and then publish it accordingly. You can also extend the story at any time. You need to make sure that the content you upload reaches your audience. If this is not the case, this completely contradicts the purpose of advertising.

Keep in mind that all subscribers on your corporate page will see the history. Stories are an easy way for most people to make a personal connection with the audience. So, remember, it's all about making a personal connection without overloading you with business issues. You need to find the perfect balance between business and personal communication. Share a few posts that are fun or easy and include them in some business-related posts.

Your Facebook followers are always on the lookout for something genuine and interesting. You are a representative of your company, but do not forget to give your audience something that captivates them. You can develop and improve your relationships with online users with Facebook Stories. To make the stories look a bit more individual, you can add selfies, post pictures of interesting events of the day, provide a quick overview of what's going on, or even add some quotes or "deep thoughts." For example, if you have a big ad or big event planned for the future, you can use Facebook Stories for daily updates.

One thing you should never forget when using advertising on Facebook is that people go to Facebook because it is fun and interesting to them. So, you need to make sure your Facebook stories meet these simple criteria. The best way to make people happy with your updates is to give them something valuable. The content needs to entertain users, offer them ideas they cannot get from anyone, share things that make them feel valuable, and show them the private side of your business that's just for Facebook Stories.

Now that you are informed about Facebook Stories, the next step is to integrate it into your advertising campaign successfully.

CHAPTER 14

FACEBOOK LIVE

Nowadays, live video has become a popular form of advertising, and Facebook has responded to that with a new tool, Facebook Live.

Facebook Live is a streaming video option from Facebook. You can stream a live video to your audience about your business profile or personal profile. Launched in April 2016, Facebook Live is very popular with online marketers and advertisers today.

Once you create a video from Facebook Live, it stays on your page or profile, so anyone who missed the live broadcast can still see it. The video will be displayed during and after the event in the user's news feed. You may be wondering why a company should use this feature. Here are a few of the reasons that will prompt you to include Facebook live video in your ad campaign:

- This helps a company to connect with its audience sincerely and gives the brand a personal feel. If you have ever felt that the audience tends to view your brand as a corporate robot, you can change that with this feature.

- You can easily interact with your users in real time and answer their questions. It allows you to interact with your viewers if they are interested.

- You can use Facebook Live to demonstrate the event to anyone who cannot attend the event. It helps you to connect with your customers and subscribers.

- You can also share industry updates.

- Facebook Live also helps you to demonstrate your corporate culture. This is the perfect way to give your brand a sense of humanity.

When should Facebook Live be used?

You need to know when you can use Facebook Live. There are certain cases where a video on Facebook Live works better than a normal post. This section offers suggestions about what to consider when using Facebook Live and when it is most appropriate.

If you want to introduce the audience to the experience of your business or brand, use Facebook Live. This only works if you have a physical storefront. It conveys the appearance of your business or employees that you cannot convey with texts or images.

Use this feature when you want to conduct events or webinars. A well-planned webinar is an easy way to reach potential customers.

This is the perfect tool for hosting a question and answer session that you want your audience to be engaged in. If you can interact with your viewers in real time, then that has more impact than normal text conversations on the Internet. When planning and reporting on a Q & A session, you can attract many of your viewers. This helps to build a better relationship.

Use Facebook Live to offer online classes. Information is the most valuable asset today. If you can provide free and valuable information, you can create a loyal audience. The public will want to visit your site more often if you can offer them something valuable.

Product release is pretty intriguing. If you are planning a product launch, do not forget to transfer it to Facebook Live. It is also a good customer service platform.

To start a Facebook live event

Now that you know what Facebook Live is, the next step is to use it. This section tells you the simple steps you need to take to get started. You will need a mobile phone or desktop with a good camera and a microphone to start a Facebook live event.

The first step is to click the "Live Video" button. If you use Facebook on your mobile phone, a small button will appear when composing a post that says "Live Video." Click here to start. If you're using the desktop, Live Video appears in the Publish window.

The next step is to write an attractive description. The description, along with the thumbnail video, is the most important parts of the video. Without convincing content, you cannot entice viewers into watching videos. When writing a copy, make sure it is direct, effective, and informative. Try to give the viewer the information he needs but hold some content back to create a sense of curiosity.

Once you've done all this, it's time to take a stand and act. If you want to record some type of series, try to be consistent with your location. You must use the same set if it is a repeating series. So, choose a place carefully.

Use an external microphone to improve sound quality.

When finished, click Finish and the stream will stop. Make sure you completed the session correctly and did not forget to stop the stream.

After the live broadcast ends, your video will continue to be broadcast to all viewers who missed the live broadcast. You can share the video on the page and even make the necessary changes to it.

Using Facebook Live with a desktop computer

If you want to use Facebook Live on your desktop, you'll need to open the browser of your choice and then visit Facebook.com.

Touch the status text box on the screen, then tap Live video.

Enter a brief description for the live video, select your privacy settings, and click "Next." When prompted, click "Allow" to grant Facebook the necessary permissions to access the webcam and microphone. After doing this, you need to click on "Go Live," and the live feed will start.

Before, during, and after Facebook Live

There are some things you need to do before, during, and after posting on Facebook Live.

First, you need to promote the event before streaming live video. It's important to understand that a live video is very similar to an event and not a blog post. You can always follow the content you posted with consistent advertising, but for live video, the action takes place before the actual event. In other words, you need to generate enough news for viewers to see the video. With Facebook, you can use your promotions to target specific events and groups. You'll need to post your upcoming ad on your Facebook page as often as possible. This means that you need to share daily broadcast updates. You need to communicate something valuable if you remind the audience of this event. Promote the live event on other social networks of your company to attract a large audience.

You must limit any distractions if you opt for Facebook Live. Yes, Facebook Live is certainly more relaxed and offers a natural experience compared to traditional advertising. However, this does not mean that you should not plan ahead of time. You need to remember that you represent the brand, and what you do in live broadcasting affects your brand and your business. That's why it's important that you always put your company's best foot forward.

You also need to make some formatting decisions. How would you like to record a video and when would you like to air it? For example, if you use the Facebook application on iOS, you can place the video horizontally or vertically as needed. Do a test video to see which feature works best for you.

Time is crucial when it comes to videos on Facebook. Send regular email alerts, notifications, or post information about an upcoming event. Your goal is to reach and attract your audience. If you plan a live event rather late at night or early in the morning, you will miss your viewers.

You must constantly offer the audience context. You may think it is enough to introduce yourself or your brand at the beginning of the video and then stop it. Do not assume that the video stream will remain in place as soon as the viewer clicks on the video stream in real time. Also, there may be other viewers who opt for later participation. To attract all viewers, you must periodically provide a context for the video.

The video has to be approachable. Live comments and reactions make the experience more interactive for the user. So, you must try your best to make the user feel like it is a two-way conversation. For the conversation to be interesting, you need to interact with the audience and respond to their comments or reactions.

You can also use this feature to announce any shout outs.

CHAPTER 15

FACEBOOK PIXELS

We highly recommend that you set up your Facebook Pixel as it is the best way to enjoy Facebook Business Manager. It is simply a set of codes that Facebook helps you to generate so when you place it on your website or on Facebook with the help of cookies, it grants you access to information to help you optimize your ads, track conversations, remarket leads, and build target audiences for ads. Facebook Pixels are of so much importance that we advise that you set it up right away, even if you are not ready to start your ad campaign yet. This is because it helps to start collecting data as soon as it is installed so by the time you are ready to start creating your ads, you will already have enough ads to work with.

The main thing these pixels do for you is that they help you get the best out of your ad campaign. They make sure that your ads reach the desired people who are most likely to take action. With this, your investments do not go to waste as you are sure of higher conversion rates.

Below are some of the ways Facebook Pixels can help you increase the results of Facebook Marketing:

Helps in tracking your Facebook conversion rates: You do not have to launch your ads and leave its success to fate because you are in the dark about how the ads are performing. With Facebook Pixels, you can track the performance of your ads by knowing about the interaction of your audience with your website after they have viewed the ads. This simply means that you will be able to track the conversion rates of your ads.

Not only can you track the activities of the ads, but you can also track the activities of customers across devices. This means that you will know whether people switch to desktop after viewing your ad on mobile or maybe if it's the other way around. This information will help you to re-evaluate your ad campaign strategy to know whether or not you need to refine it. Also, it will be easier for you to calculate your return on investment.

Facebook Retargeting: There are some customers that have already interacted with your site through your ads but haven't taken any marketing action. These are the one that your retargeting ads are for. With the help of Facebook retargeting data and dynamic ads, you will be able to reach customers who have shown interest in certain products on your site. For example, if someone already visited your website and added a product to their wish list or cart, your retargeting ads will have to be that of the product they are interested in. This is a way of reminding your potential customers that their preferred products are waiting for them so they can come for it when they are ready.

Creates lookalike audiences: Facebook can help you expand your audience by helping you to reach people who have the same likes, interests, and demographics with those that are already interacting with your website. Through this, you will get more people to know your brand and some of these people will certainly convert into real customers.

Optimize your ads to increase conversions: You can use the data provided by Facebook tracking pixel to boost your ads for particular conversion events on your website. Without a tracking pixel, you will only be able to optimize conversions like click links. Pixels, however, help you to optimize those conversions that align closely with the goals of your business.

Optimize your ads for value: This is made possible by the data Facebook collects on those that buy from your website through Facebook and how much they have spent on the site. This data can help you optimize your ads' audience based on their value. What this means is that Facebook will show your ads to those customers that are likely to make big purchases.

Grants you access to more Facebook tools and Metrics: The only way you can get to use some Facebook tools is by installing Facebook Pixels. For example, if you want to use custom audiences for your website, web conversion campaigns, or dynamic ads, you will need Facebook Pixel. In addition to this, Pixels helps you to know the cost of your campaign by tracking metrics like cost per conversion or cost per leads.

A Guide on Using Facebook Pixels

Now that you already know the great benefits that Facebook Pixels has, it is time to learn how to put this tool to great use.

Here are ways you can use Facebook pixels to gather data on two different kinds of events (specific actions that your website's visitors take on the site), these are:

Facebook standard events, which are the platform's predefined set of 17 standard events.

Customized events which you have set up yourself.

Facebook Pixel's 17 Standard Events

Below are 17 predetermined Facebook pixel events whose codes you can simply copy and paste:

Purchase: Someone who has successfully made a purchase on your site.

Lead: A person who has signed up for a trial or on the other hand, identified themselves as a leader on your page.

Complete Registration: For a person that has successfully completed a registration form like a subscription form on your site.

Add Payment Information: When someone adds their payment information on the website, in the process of making a purchase.

Add to Cart: When a person adds your product to their shopping cart on your website.

Add to Wishlist: A person includes a product to their wishlist on your website.

Initiate Checkout: Anyone who begins the process of checking out to buy something on your website.

Search: Anybody who makes use of the search function on your website to look for a particular product on the site.

View Content: When a person lands on a specific page on your website.

Contact: Someone who reaches out to your business.

Customize Product: Someone selects a specific variant of a preferred product.

Donate: When a person gives freely to your cause..

Find Location: When someone initiates a search for the physical location of your business.

Schedule: Anyone who books an appointment with your business.

Start Trial: A person who signs up for a free trial period of your product.

Submit Application: A person applies for any of your products, services, or events.

Subscribe: When a person completes a subscription for a paid product or service.

Also, you can add extra codes known as parameters to add details to standard events. This will help you to customize standard events based on currency, basket contents, content type/ID, and the worth of conversion event.

Facebook Pixel's Custom Events

Custom Events is a feature that helps you get more details than those provided by Facebook Pixel's standard events or to customize events to suit the peculiar needs of your website in place of standard events. These types of events make use of URL rules which depends on the rules of specific URLs or URL keywords.

To create custom events in place of standard events, go to the 'Custom Conversion Section', then click on 'Create Custom Conversion'. Add the URL or part of the URL already copied from your website, which represents your custom event. In a case where you are making use of URL Equals, ensure that you also add the domain e.g. 'www'. It is unnecessary for you to include 'HTTP' or 'https'.

If you are using a different analytics tool, take a look at the list of your page views there, then copy and paste the exact URL.

Once this is done, the next thing you should do is to select a category and click 'Next'.

You are expected to give a unique name to your custom event and provide a description of it. If applicable, you should also add a conversion value. Note, however, that our conversion values are expected to be in whole numbers, without additional characters like the dollar sign. Including conversion values helps you to keep track of your ROI. Once you have entered all necessary pieces of information, click 'Done'. You can now create your ad using the objective of your website conversion by selecting the custom event you want to optimize, then track that event.

Split Standard events with Custom Conversions

If you discover that you need more customization when you are already using standard events, you can help yourself out with custom conversions. For example, if you have a shoe line and you are already using the View Content standard events for your products but want to optimize for different categories, you can do this using custom events. When doing this, apply the same rules for URL create conversions for our different categories.

P.S.: In case the URL rules do not apply to your website, you can use events to create custom conversions and add parameters.

Creating Facebook Pixels to Add to your Website

Now that we are done learning what we can track on our website using Facebook Pixels and why we would want to track them, let us now consider creating these pixels and putting them to work on our websites.

To create Facebook pixels, click on Business Settings' on your Business Manager Dashboard, choose 'Pixels' on the 'People and Assets' tab on the left-hand side then click 'Add'.

You will now give a name to your pixel, by entering no less than 50 characters on the space provided, then click create. Before you create, make sure you go through Pixels' terms and conditions because you are agreeing to them once you use the service.

Wait for a moment for your pixel to be created then click on 'Set up the Pixel Now'.

The last step to take in creating your Facebook pixels is to follow the detailed instructions on your Facebook pixel guide carefully, to start collecting data by setting up pixels on your website.

Keep in mind that Facebook allows you to create ten pixels when you are using Facebook Business Manager.

Create your First Ad Campaign on Facebook Business Manager

Now that you have successfully set up your pixels, you can now create your first ad with confidence that it will do relatively well.

To create an ad, click on 'Business Manager' at the top left-hand side of your Business Manager Dashboard. There, you will see the 'Create and 'Manage' tab, click the ads manager then click on the green 'Create' button.

You will receive a pop-up, and there, select 'Guided Creation' then choose the objective of your campaign, target it to an audience, set budget and schedule, and choose your preferred type of ads according to the different types of ads.

There you have it! With these steps, you are now ready to make the most out of Facebook with everything you need in one spot, to get the greatest results out of your ads and other Facebook marketing efforts, thanks to Facebook Business Manager. Let us now take a critical look at Facebook advertising to know the best ways to tweak your ads, the best industry practices, as well as some dos and don'ts to get ample results from your ad campaigns.

CHAPTER 16

SCHEDULING

Controlling when ads are delivered

You are going to be able to control how your ads are delivered and when they are going to run.

Your ad is going to be eligible to start being posted as soon as it is approved. This process is usually going to take up to twenty four hours but for some ads it could take longer. If you decide to have your ad posted as soon as it is approved, then it is going to start running once the review process is over.

Another option that you can use is to have your ad run at a specific time. You will create your ads and then turn off the ad set or the campaign. Therefore, once the ad is reviewed and approved, you can turn it on whenever you are ready to start having your ad delivered.

A third option would be to create a schedule while you are creating the ad. In order to do this, you are going to pick start and stop dates in the scheduling section. This will tell facebook when to deploy your ad and when to pull it off the site. In order to schedule your ad to be run at certain times or days of the wekk you will have to be using the lifetime budget and then you are going to follow these steps.

1. Go to the ad scheduling section in your ad set creation.

2. Go to run ads on a schedule.

3. You may have to click on the advance options first

4. Find the dropdown that allows you to pick your schedules time zone. This is going to need to be in your timezone so that you can know exactly when it is going to be deployed.

5. You also can view reports for time of day ad account time zone or ad time of day viewer's time zone.

6. Pick the time of day and the days of the week that you are going to want your ad to show.

7. Finish making your ad and place your order.

Viewing and editing ad schedules

In order to go in and look at the times and dates that you have set your ad to run you will.

1. Open the ads manager or power editor

2. Select which campaign you are wanting to use

3. Go to the ad set and move over to the schedule column.

4. In order to edit this schedule you will

5. Open up the ad manager or power editor and move over to the ad that you are wanting to edit.

6. Click on edit and make your changes.

7. Make sure to hit save so that your changes can be applied.

Managing delivery

You are going to pick between two delivery systems for your ads; either standard or accelerated. You can find the choice under the delivery type in your budget and schedule section when you are creating your ad. Most ads are going to want to use the standard delivery so that the budget that is set for that ad can be spread out throughout the entire campaign and the ad reaches out to the most people possible. But, those people who are working with bigger budgets are going to want to reach out to as many people as quickly as possible will choose the accelerated delivery.

When you are using the accelerated delivery you will:

1. Use manual bidding in order for you to be in control of the maximum price for the delivery of the ad. The maximum cost bidding has to be chosen so that facebook can optimize the budget that they are given rather than worry about trying

to save money and get the ad seen more.

2. The ad is still going to have to go through the review process.

3. The ad duration should be set to at least two hours so that more people can be reached and there is enough time for the ad to be delivered. Campaigns that have lower time frames are going to experience under delivery.

4. Being that accelerated delivery is going to go for speed and not value, there is probably going to be a higher cost per result. While using the accelerated option is going to prevent people from getting the most raw value, it is going to be worth it because the ad could be tied to a time sensitive sale that is not going to be going on later.

5. Whenever you are using the accelerated option the entire budget for your ad will be spent as quickly as possible. This means that your budget could be spent before the end of your campaign and if that happens, the ad is no longer going to be delivered.

Ad set end dates

The end date is going to tell the facebook system when an ad needs to stop being delivered. Having to pick an end date is going to depend on what type of budget that you are going to use.

If you are going to use a lifetime budget, then you will have to pick an end date so that the budget can be spent at an even pace and your ad is seen by as many people in your target audience as possible.

The daily budget will allow you to set an end date but it is not required. If you do not then the ad will continue to be delivered until you interfere and pause it or untile the account spending limit has been reached.

Note: the end date for your ad can be changed at any time, but it is not recommended to be done too often because that will interfere with the delivery system.

CHAPTER 17

CHARGES

Cost to advertise on Facebook, Instagram, and an Audience Network

Whenever you begin advertising you can pick from a daily or lifetime budget as well as picking how much you want to spend on the entire campaign. Many ads are going to range between a dollar to five dollars a day, but you are probably going to need to spend more in order to reach out to more people.

The budget is going to work with the audience you are trying to target and the type of bidding that you choose in order to determine how many people will see and click on your ad. In order to find out how much of your budget, audience, and bid is going to affect the outcome, you will be able to use a facebook tool to calculate.

Boosted posts

To boost a post you will go to your page and select the boost post button. Then you will pick your targeting preferences, your budget, and look to see about how many people facebook thinks are going to see your ad with the budget that you are using. If you do not want to go on, you are going to click cancel, if you do, then you will hit next and walk through the steps to order a boosted post.

Ad creation

You also have the option of using ad creation. When you use ad creation you are going to be picking an objective and looking at how many people you are potentially going to reach. You will then pick your schedule and budget so that you can look at how much you are expected to reach in a day.

Impressions

You cannot pay for anything except impressions because of two things.

1. The objective that you have selecting is only going to be able to charge you for impressions.

2. You are creating a new ad and you have to spend at least ten dollars for impressions before you can pick something else. This is done so that the integrity of the account can be tested.

CHAPTER 18

REACHING YOUR CORE AUDIENCE

Ad targeting

Whenever you are picking a target audience for your ad, you can create a new audience or you can use one that has already been saved.

Creating a new audience

You will find this option when you are in the audience section of the ad set creation.

1. Location: this will target an audience in a specific location. This can be narrowed down to zip code or to a specific country.

2. Age: this will target people inside of a set age range

3. Gender: men, women, or both.

4. Languages: people who speak specific languages will be targeted. So if you want to target someone who speaks Spanish, you will have the option to only show your ad to Spanish speaking people.

5. Detailed targeting: you can exclude people from your target because of interests, behaviors, or demographics.

6. Custom audiences: you will create a custom audience based on specific sources that you are wanting to be targeted. It is most commonly used for finding people who are similar to those who are in your source.

You can mix and match your options as it fits your audience. But you should not use too many at once. This can lead up to an audience that cannot be found, or is too small to be effective. You should keep in mind that in any target audience that you create,

Facebook is going to automatically try to find the people that are going to produce the best results. That is why you do not want to refine too much.

Your potential reach will be the number of people who are in your targeted audience. You are going to be able to increase or decrease this number by changing the boarders of your target area. The estimated daily reach will be how many people will be reached in a given day.

Note

1. Numbers that you see for how many people you are going to reach a day is going to be an estimate only. They cannot be used in helping you decide how much you can spend on an ad and is definitely not a guarantee of how many people are going to see your ad.

2. You are going to be able to find the numbers for how many are in your targeted area or your estimated rach will found in the audience definition section which can be found to the right of the ad creation options.

3. Because of how many people are advertising on Facebook, things are constantly being improved so that numbers are more accurate.

4. The number estimates are going to be based off of several different factors such as ads that are similar and how they worked with targeting.

Saved audience

You will have to save the audience before you you can use it on a different set of ads. In order to do this create your audience and select the save this audience button located at the bottom of the audience section.

Note: whenever an audience is saved, everything about it will be saved for future use except for the location. You will have to select the location you are targeting each time that it is used.

In order to use a saved audience you will pick the saved audience button which can be found at the top of the audience section.

Note: if you are making modifications to your audience, then you are going to click on the edit button which will allow you to make changes to the already saved audience. You will be able to get to these modifications in your audience page.

Setting your target audience

You are going to want to look at your target audience in two different ways. You can target them specifically or you can target them broadly.

Specific targeting

When you use specific targeting you are going to be giving relatively strict parameters in order for Facebook to locate the best people to show the ad to. These parameters are going to be used for targeting demographics, or lookalike audiences. You may even be able to have a potential audience that is smaller but is audience that is smaller but also interested in what you are advertising

Broad targeting

When you target broadly you are going to be relying on the delivery system of Facebook to locate the best people to show your ad to. With this approach, you are going to be finding potential customers that you would have known about. If you are going to target broadly, then you will want to check the audience insights or ads reporting so that you can figure out the type of people that are being found for you.

Neither targeting type is going to be better than the other. And, you are not going to be able to use both types in order to send out your ads. The delivery system offered by Facebook is going to optimize the result that you are wanting no matter how specific your audience is. The less targeting parameters that you use, the broader the approach will be.

CHAPTER 19

FACEBOOK STATISTICS THAT MATTER FOR MARKETERS IN 2019

- Out of Facebook's monthly users, 66% or 1.47 billion people use it on a daily basis.

- People's visit to Facebook lasts for ten to 12 minutes.

- 88% of Facebook users access it through their mobile devices.

- Facebook is still the biggest social media platform in the world.

- Facebook Messenger is the most downloaded app.

- There are 80 million small- and medium-sized business pages on Facebook.

- Facebook revenue is twice what it was three years ago due to a 42% increase it gets every year.

- 89% of B2B businesses use Facebook.

- 30% of Facebook's ad audience are aged 25 to 30 years old, and 7.35% are below the age of 25.

- 270 million people in India use Facebook, thus making it the largest population of people on the platform. This is followed by America with 210 million users, which makes up 10% of global Facebook users.

- About 1.1 billion or 50% of Facebook users speak English, while the other half speaks more than 100 languages.

- There are one billion group members on Facebook with 200 million people belonging to meaningful Facebook Groups.

- Facebook offers the highest ROI on digital ads compared to other social media platforms.

- 3.91% is the rate of average engagement for a post.

- In the second quarter of 2019, the average price of an ad increased by 17%.

- Over 24% of Facebook pages use Facebook ad.

- Roughly 50% of Facebook users click on eight ads in a month.

- 71% of people on Facebook now engage in online video viewing, while 60% more are expected to do so this year.

- 24.5% of all paid video ads on social media belong to Facebook in 2018.

- About 150 million people are getting familiar with the new Facebook stories feature.

- The highest traffic recorded is between 1:00 to 3:00 in the afternoon on weekdays, so it is also the best time for you to advertise your products or services.

- Engagement is 18% higher on Thursdays and Fridays.

All You Need to Know About Facebook Video Ads for 2019

Using Facebook ads is one of the best ways to engage with people in your page and get traffic for your website. Because of that, your video ads need to be interesting and easy to remember as well. Here are some ideas on how you can make that happen.

Catch viewers' attention early

When you're watching a video ad for the first time and clicks away within seconds, it's a sign that you're not getting what you want. If you don't want your target audience to do the same with your advertisement, you should try to grab the viewers' attention and get the message across from the start of the clip to stop them from disregarding your ad.

Ensure that it's mobile-friendly

Making your video advertisement accessible via mobile should be your main priority since 95% of Facebook users open the platform through their smartphones and tablets. So, think of the size of the screen they may use, the sound, as well as the duration of the clip.

Make it as short as possible

You can easily convert viewers into buyers with shorter videos. Facebook recommends a length of five to 15 seconds for in-stream and standalone video ads. You should also mention your brand in the first three seconds on the advertisement so that people won't forget about it. It cannot be considered as spam if you utter the business name several times in that short clip as well. The viewers know that it's an advertisement; that's why it is expected and forgivable to do that.

Use engaging ad title and description

You need an engaging title and description to inform your audience of what they should look forward to see in the video. People become curious when your title is catchy enough or you use funny statements. It does not suffice to say, "Watch it; you'll learn something from it." Everyone is after increasing their knowledge, but no one wants to be told that they lack in that department.

Consider the recommended aspect ratio

When you use the normal aspect ratio of 9:16 and 1:1, you're making it easier for your potential clients to view your video. The only devices that people use to watch something is their desktop computer and smartphone. By producing the clip in both ratios, it will be effortless for the viewers to continue playing the video even when they flip their mobile phone.

Attach your CTA in the middle of your ad

Promote your call to action in the middle of your video ad if you want your users to take a particular action. It is a recommended technique since people sometimes like taking action at once instead of waiting for more details. Not everyone honestly has time to watching something all day, so you cannot miss out on that opportunity.

Its downside, however, is that the ad might convert less as the viewers may not watch the video to the last second. They already got what they were looking for; that's why it won't bother them even if they do not see the end of the clip.

Choose the right Facebook ad objective

Whatever you wish to achieve with your ad should be clear throughout the video. Your brand awareness is more important than anything if you want more people to remember your business, for one. If your goal is to encourage them to visit your site and generate more sales, you can select "Traffic" and "Conversations," respectively.

Understand your KPIs

After knowing the reason why you're creating your ad, you need to choose the key performance indicators for your campaign to figure out how successful it is.

Use the right Facebook video ad specs

One of the things that can make or break your ad is its specifications. The recommended resolution for videos on Facebook is 1080 pixels. The length can range from one second to four hours as long as it does not exceed the maximum size of 4GB. Of course, it should look like a professional director create it as well. You have to upload a high-quality clip to keep folks from scrolling past the advertisement.

Match your objective to your Facebook video ad types

There are many options for video ad formats that you can select from to convey your message in the best possible way. For instance, you may use Facebook Stories, in-stream ads, canvas ads, sponsored live videos, video carousel ads, vertical video ads, and GIFs. When choosing any of them, though, ensure that the format is in line with your marketing objectives.

- You can use a short format like a vertical video ad or GIF if you simply want to increase your video's views or direct more people towards your content.

- Video carousel and in-stream ads are options you should think of if your aim is to increase brand awareness.

- Use a sponsored video if you'd like people to react to your video by liking, sharing or making a comment on it.

- You can use the collection ads when you create a video that will increase your sales and conversion rate.

Hit your target

By improving your video ad targeting, you'll be increasing your ROI even if you already have a particular marketing objective. Most often, Facebook video ad targeting is almost the same as Facebook ad targeting as a whole. After all, similar audiences can sometimes be a very great way of getting your videos ads to the right crowd that will most likely be interested in them.

Also, with Facebook, you can set up custom audiences with users that have viewed your video ads in the past and retarget them since you already know that they have watched your clips willingly before.

Using Facebook Messenger to Grow Your Business

In the next few years, the majority of customer-business interactions will be done through technology, particularly on messaging apps. With more than 1.3 million users monthly, Facebook Messenger is one of the largest platforms of the same type in existence. For this reason, every serious business owner should start working on their marketing strategy, reaching out to their customers, and interacting with them personally through the app.

Facebook Messenger Tools for Business

Just like WhatsApp Business, Facebook Messenger comes with

different tools that can help you as a business owner to keep your various threads under control.

Messenger Greetings

These are customizable messages that automatically show up when someone starts a chat with a seller/business for the first time.

Instant Replies

These are similar to Messenger Greetings. The only difference is that it is a quick reply to a user's question. They are also automatically designed to provide a response to anyone that sends a message to your business. Instant replies are pre-made messages that you can program to give answers to common questions like contact information or business hours.

Customer Cards

Customer cards provide information about the consumer that contacted you in order to craft the best response by looking at the customer's local time, location, et cetera.

Why You Should Use Facebook Messenger for Business

Facebook Messenger can be used by businesses, especially small companies, in different ways. When you communicate with customers through the app, the service becomes personalized, and they feel that you genuinely care about them. In time, it can lead to an increase in your profits.

A lot of consumers tend to contact customer service representatives through a written message than a phone call because the issues get resolved within a few seconds when communicated through Messenger. Also, people prefer doing businesses with businesses that they can contact directly; that's why you need to be active on this platform. If you aren't available for 24 hours, let people know about your working schedule or when you'll come back to attend to their needs. This way, they have an idea of when to and not to message you, as well as the date or time when they can expect to receive your response.

Facebook Messenger Ads

Using Facebook Messenger ads is a tremendous opportunity to get the most out of your advertising budget. Work on creating conversations that your customers can relate with and give them reasons to continue interacting with your business on the app.

For the mobile platform, click-to-Messenger ads can now be placed on the Messenger home screen or Facebook. The icon shows on your ad, which may be in the form of a video, image or carousel.

The proper CTA button for this type of ad should be "Send a Message" or "Learn More," and you have the option of creating a greeting while producing your ad. So, when someone clicks the latter, a chat box will pop up, and the consumer can start sending questions about the merchandise you are promoting.

You can also create ads that will be placed directly on the home screen of your mobile Messenger so that, when people click on it, they'll be sent to your landing page.

Furthermore, sponsored messages can be used on your Messenger to re-market and re-engage people who have interacted with your business before or those that have bought from you. They are great for last-minute sales updates and reminders as they are usually sent to existing threads.

The Future of Facebook Messenger for Business

Small businesses need to take advantage of Facebook Messenger marketing as technologies will continue to grow in the years to come. About 100,000 chatbots are available on the platform today, and they can act as your personal assistant and make use of artificial intelligence. Businesses can also incorporate them to their services and improve brand awareness and sales. As soon as small businesses can have their personal chatbot add-ons, they'll be able to advertise their products and services through the app.

CHAPTER 20

MORE WAYS TO USE FACEBOOK FOR MARKETING

The value of Facebook for marketing cannot be exaggerated. Among all the other social media platforms, Facebook holds the number 1 spot. It is not just a place for friends to connect, it is also a venue for brands to promote themselves and interact with their clientele. It doesn't matter if you are a big business or a small brand, you can use a Facebook fan page to make yourself known, increase your audience reach and build customer relations.

Here are some ways you can use Facebook for marketing and promotions

Use the Facebook fan page to create awareness for your brand identity.

Conventional marketing strategies make clients familiar with business brands through product and services listings. With Facebook, you can promote your brand through a customizable page that expresses your business's unique character. You can share posts, images, videos and links that show your personality. Compared to formal business websites, a Facebook page is more personal and can express your human side. People will easily identify with you because you are not just a business who is trying to take consumers' money.

You can be flexible when it comes to creating brand awareness and affinity through Facebook. The posts you share can either be related to your product and services or not at all, as long as you are connecting with people and not diverting away from your company's philosophies and core values. You can share funny videos, viral posts, educational references and the likes.

Use Facebook Ads.

Similar to classified ads in newspapers, Facebook has its own way of promoting brands. When you advertise, your ad will be seen on the side column of the social media site. These ads include the following features:

- Headline
- Copy
- Image
- Click-through link to your Facebook page, official website or an app.

When you have an advertisement on the side column, you are increasing your chances of page visits, website clicks and possible likes.

When you use Facebook Ads, you will be able to do the following:

- Target particular audience according to demographics. You can utilize information such as age, gender, and interests among others.
- Set your own budgets for advertisements. These can be on a daily, weekly or monthly basis.
- Test ads. You can run multiple versions of your ads at the same time. You will be able to compare your setups and designs and see which is more effective.
- You can measure your own ads using Facebook Ad's built-in tools.

When you use Facebook Advertising, you increase the likelihood of generating "Like" on your page. Once a user likes you page, they automatically become followers and your posts will be visible on their newsfeed. When they like your post, that event will be visible on their friends' newsfeeds. This means more interaction and further reach which may mean possible conversions.

Host promotions, sweepstakes and contests on Facebook.

Like conventional marketing, promotions can boost brand awareness. You will be using a third-party app to make a contest and direct participants to your Facebook page. The reliable contests are not simply asking for participants to like your page or writing a comment. If you want their entries and your contest to be valid, use other tools and contest templates. There are free tools like Shortstack and Pagemodo but you can also use a lot of paid tools.

Use promoted posts.

By paying a flat rate, Facebook will allow you to have promoted posts that reach specific number of users. This ensures that your follower and fans ALWAYS see your post on their newsfeed. When you don't use promoted posts, the chances are high that your post will be swamped by others and you will lose visibility. Additionally, Promoted Posts also allow you to the friends of your fans.

You can set up Promoted Posts with just a click of a button. You don't have to worry about computing how much you pay on a daily, weekly, or monthly basis because it comes with a flat rate. However, it does not include the options for targeting that you can use with Facebook Ads.

Use Facebook Sponsored Stories.

This is all about word-of-mouth advertising. Sponsored Stories encourage users to imitate the action of their friends on Facebook. For instance, if a friend likes a page, then he will think it is a reliable or interesting site and will like it as well. If a friend claims an offer from a Facebook page, the user may also be enticed to do the same. Even if the friend has liked the page a long time ago, the user will still see it on his news feed and on the right column. This way, the post does not get overlooked.

Sponsored Stories can also be utilized with Facebook's Open Graph. For example, a friend has just played and installed a particular game on Facebook, the app will send an invitation to challenge friends to play the same game. Sponsored Stories are easy to create and customize.

Use Facebook Open Graph

Effective marketing relies on studying your client's reactions and interactions. The same is true with Facebook. You can see billions of different kinds of user interactions daily using Open Graph. This helps you identify other creative options that you can utilize for your posts.

Third party apps often prompt users to register using their Facebook accounts and it automatically connects them to Open Graph. Once they sign-up or login using Facebook, the app requests permission to other applications. Usually the user just clicks through this without giving it much thought. This way, the apps are able to stream information onto other friends' newsfeeds, such as what song the user is listening to, what movie he is watching, what game he is playing, etc. This gives the friends various options like action, do the same action or share it. It capitalizes on consumer story, like a testimonial.

What makes Open Graph actions effective as marketing tools is that they are more meaningful. When a familiar friend is sort of promoting the brand in a particular way, users are encouraged to take action.

Use Facebook Exchange

Ad retargeting is possible with Facebook. Businesses can analyze web history data and see when a user has visited their webpage but did not make a purchase. If this is the case, they post an advertisement for the same product to reach the same user to encourage him to click that Buy button. It is interesting to note that FBX can also appear in newsfeeds aside from side columns.

With all these amazing ways you can advertise, Facebook is the best social media network to promote your product, service or brand.

CHAPTER 21

TIPS FOR 2019 AND BEYOND

Facebook is a worldwide powerhouse with regards to web-based social networking showcasing. It was the main informal community to discharge advertisements and albeit most other interpersonal organizations could never let it be known, Facebook set the standard for how promotions are kept running on informal communities. It does not shock anyone that numerous organizations rely upon Facebook for their promoting needs.

Obviously, much the same as any advertising stage, Facebook has its good and bad times. Just as of late, Facebook started diminishing the impact of business promotions on newsfeed to reinforce social communication and significant associations. You can check the Facebook Newsroom on the off chance that you wish to become familiar with the issue.

In spite of the ongoing changes, Facebook is as yet the top web based life organize for organizations hoping to extend their compass. As per "Statista," there are over 2.234 billion month to month dynamic Facebook clients from everywhere throughout the world as of the second quarter of 2018. . No other informal organization can pull off these sorts of numbers. All things considered, given the ongoing difficulties, it could easily compare to ever for organizations to guarantee that they are doing Facebook showcasing right if just to make the most out of what the informal community brings to the table as far as advancing one's item or administration.

Here are ten hints that you can execute in your Facebook advertising methodology to advance and develop your business.

1. Ensure that you have the correct business page on Facebook

You need a legitimate business page and not an individual profile to advertise a business on Facebook adequately. This may appear glaringly evident, however numerous web-based social networking experts are frequently astounded what number of advertisers get this part off-base. Additionally, you have to ensure that your Facebook business page falls under the correct characterization from the accompanying six sorts:

- Local business or spot
- Artist, band or open figure
- Company, association or organization
- Entertainment
- Brand or item
- Cause or network

Picking the correct class is indispensable as explicit highlights could conceivably be accessible to you would it be a good idea for you to pick the wrong classification? For instance, choosing "neighbourhood business or spot" gives you an alternative to set a physical location while classifications like "Brand or item" does not have that include.

2. Enhance your pictures

You have to ensure that you set up some quality pictures on your Facebook business page. Interpersonal organizations can be incredibly visual and more when you are doing Facebook advertising. From the profile picture, spread photographs and updates — all pictures ought to be as enamouring as could be expected under the circumstances and pass on to individuals what it is that your business does.

3. Utilize the CTA (Call to Action) catch

Another component that numerous advertisers will in general neglect while doing web based showcasing office through the Facebook informal organization is to incorporate a straightforward CTA catch on each business page. In the event that you don't have one all through your site, at that point you are leaving a lot of cash on the table.

What the CTA catch says and does depends altogether on how you set it up and you have no lack of alternatives — Shop Now, Sign Up, Contact Us, Use App, See Video and the sky is the limit from there. You can interface these catches to your point of arrival, a contact structure, a video that you might want to advance or a pick in page. Everything relies upon what you are hoping to achieve with your Facebook business page.

4. Begin normally posting "adjusted" content

Since you have your Facebook business page all together, the time has come to make content for clients. Try not to restrict yourself to only one kind of substance and grasp the chance to explore different avenues regarding various arrangements to see which mix your gathering of people prefers best.

On the off chance that you are thinking that its hard to stir up your substance and drawing in your gathering of people, you can generally begin with the 70-20-10 propensity:

Publish unique material 70 percent of the time

Post content important to the enthusiasm of your group of onlookers 20 percent of the time

Create self-special substance just 10 percent of the time

In the event that you pass by the guidelines referenced above, you would almost certainly stir up your substance and never keep running into the issue of exhausting your group of onlookers. All the more critically, it opens up a chance to voice our worries and express your perceptions in your specialty.

5. Enhance your posts

On the off chance that the motivation behind your online networking update is to share a connection, ensure that you dispense with the connection URL from the post. To do as such, essentially glue the connection and give Facebook a couple of moments to catch the data about the URL (picture, title, and first section) and after that erase the URL before posting. Doing as such will help because your post to seem less jumbled and help drive centre to the subject and picture of your post. In the event that you should share interface outside of what Facebook gives, you can utilize Google URL Shortened to make the activity look cleaner and increasingly shareable.

6. Influence client produced content

In Facebook advertising, you don't need to make your substance constantly. Now and then, you can share content made by your group of onlookers. Doing as such spares you time and exertion as well as similarly help advance brand devotion as you make clients feel valued that they are adding to your motivation.

Among the clearest strategies to get client created content is to solicit clients to share photographs from their involvement with your item or administration. You can likewise share posts on your locale page when one of your fans or adherents makes reference to your business. The vast majority love acknowledgment notwithstanding when it is via web-based networking media with their preferred brands setting aside the effort to thank and include them.

7. Post recordings all the more frequently

Another incredible method to expand commitment in online life is through recordings. Clients watch more than 100 million hours of video on Facebook once a day, and that is just the start. Facebook is additionally causing acclimations to how to their calculation decides singular enthusiasm through the recordings that clients are viewing.

There are some fundamental things to hold up under as a primary concern when you're creating recordings for Facebook:

- 85% of Facebook clients favor watching recordings on quiet. This suggests subtitling your recordings will be crucial to commitment.

- 80% of clients are disturbed when recordings auto-plays on their newsfeed, so ensure that you're setting up your recordings effectively when you post.

- Take preferred position of "Facebook Live" on the off chance that you are not enthused about delivering your recordings. The last is a gushing administration that gives you a chance to communicate live recordings straight from your cell phone. Numerous organizations have discovered that it is a superb method to make leads and augment commitment.

8. Use Facebook Page Insights to Monitor Progress

Normal Facebook refreshes are just a large portion of the fight. The other half is tied in with observing your measurements to find drifts in commitment so you know precisely what you are doing well (and what you are fouling up). The best apparatus for this activity is Facebook's inside examination instrument called the Facebook Page Insights.

Page Insights gives clients a reasonable picture of how your business page was doing in the course of the most recent week with subtleties of the accompanying:

- Number of page likes/not at all like

- Post Reach

- Engagement

- Comments

- Shares

9. Time your posts effectively

You ought to likewise consider the planning of your Facebook posts. Relatively few individuals understand this, yet there is such an incredible concept as the most perfect time when presenting refreshes as contradicted on just arbitrarily dropping substance on your Facebook page. So how would you do only that?

You can get data on the best occasions to distribute a Facebook post by means of your Page Insights screen. To get to this element, click on the "Bits of knowledge" tab at the highest point of your Facebook business page.

The Insights screen indicates you everything that you have to know to time your posts accurately which incorporates the accompanying:

The time when the vast majority of your Facebook supporters are on the web

How well a specific bit of substance does for the duration of the day

- Information on which of your posts is making the most commitment.

You can utilize the data referenced above to get experiences on the best time to draw in your clients. You may endeavour to distribute different material (easy-going diversion posts, etc) at various occasions of the day to perceive how it influences commitment. By learning the best time to post, you can amplify go after pretty much everything that you do when promoting your business on Facebook.

10. Exploit Audience Insights

To wrap things up on the rundown of investigation instruments that you can use for Facebook showcasing is Audience Insights. As the name recommends, Audience Insights gives you insights concerning your clients. You should simply pick a crowd of people and the page gives you socioeconomics, for example, age, sexual orientation, dimension of training and calling. Such data can demonstrate valuable for revealing the intrigue and side interests of your intended interest group. Thus, you will have a smart thought of what themes and sort of substance a large portion of your crowd find captivating.

Regardless of the amount Facebook may change its calculations, one thing is without a doubt — the interpersonal organization will stay to be a practical promoting stage for a long time to come. The way to progress is to continue improving your methodology, and you can begin with the tips referenced above and ensure that you have the situation taken care of.

FACEBOOK MARKETING PITFALLS TO AVOID

More than just doing the "right" things for Facebook marketing success, it's also important to avoid making crucial mistakes that can sabotage your efforts. Sometimes, a single and seemingly honest mistake is all it takes to render all the right things that you did worthless and make your Facebook marketing campaigns come crashing down to Earth.

BEING ABSORBED BY THE BUSYNESS

As mentioned earlier, Facebook marketing is a relatively complex activity that involves several different activities. One of the risks of such is getting stuck in activities that take up so much of your time but account for a smaller portion of results. These activities include among others constantly modifying your personal and brand or business' page and being too obsessed with data that you review and analyze them almost every hour.

While such things are truly important to your Facebook marketing success, overdoing it can be counterproductive. You'll need to exercise moderation and balance so that you can also allot enough meaningful time to other important aspects of your campaign. You may be able to interpret and analyze the data well but if you don't spend enough time writing great advertising copies or posts on Facebook, you won't be able to act on whatever important insights you can glean from data analysis.

GOING AFTER THE LATEST CRAZE

With the rapid advances in technology these days, don't be surprised to find that new and "better" tools and strategies coming out every 6 months or so. Expect that hot new thing that's the craze today to be passé by that time.

Even if such new and popular releases can be very useful, it doesn't necessarily mean it's best for your campaigns. Simply adapting the latest and trendy developments for the sake of being "current" or "relevant" isn't the point. It's all about whether or not adapting such can be significantly beneficial for your brand or business' Facebook marketing campaign or not. If adapting the latest strategies or technologies will help your campaign much more successful, go ahead and do so. But if not, don't.

CONTENT AND PROMOTIONS

One of the worst – and common – mistakes many Facebook marketers make is not giving their Facebook posts and promotions much thought, if any at all. Many campaigns have been ruined because they post and promos were simply based on what they felt like posting and promoting or on what's currently trendy at the time.

The best way to populate your business or brand's page or ads with great content is to consider your overall promotion – bigger picture thinking and being strategic. Your content must be able to give your audience value and address their concerns and questions in ways that make them want to get in on your planned or current promotions.

If for example you're a tax consultant. The month before tax season begins, your brand's page must feature content – through posts or ads – that features or points to your page's helpful tax-related tips and advice. By the end of the month, you can announce – either via posts or paid ads – that you're available to help them out with their tax-related needs, just in time for the tax season. Your content in the month leading up to tax season points your audience to your services.

CHASING THE WIND

One of the worst mistakes that can prove to be costly for you in terms of resources and time is going after the wrong crowd. For example, if you were selling fixed gear bikes, it wouldn't make sense to go after mountain bikers or road bikers, eh? But you can innocently make that mistake by being active in biking forums that have generally more non-fixed gear bikers and promoting your business page there. You can also make the same mistake by simply indicating "bikes" in the interests portion of your Facebook ads. It's too general and you run the risk of having your ads shown mostly to bikers who aren't even aware that fixed-gear bikes actually exist.

The best way to avoid this mistake is by paying close attention to details, particularly demographics and their interests, and not going after the latest and hottest trends for the sake of relevance. The more you know your audience, the better focused your campaigns will be and the higher your chances for succeeding in your Facebook marketing campaigns.

CONCLUSION

It has been a wonderful journey taking you through everything you need to know about Facebook Marketing to earn you conversions. Certainly, there are best industry practices and there are some not-so-popular ones that are capable of working magic for you, we hope you have been able to grasp it all.

The essence of this book is to make sure Facebook Marketers grasp proper knowledge of the best ways to go about their Facebook marketing journey. From the first chapter to the last, we have made a conscious effort to take you through every step you need to take in this interesting, albeit complicated, journey of marketing with the Facebook platform. From the beginning of your Facebook Marketing campaign, which starts with you creating a Facebook page, to knowing your way around Facebook Business manager, to Facebook Insights, which is the home of every activity that takes place on your Facebook page, this is a one-of-a-kind book that lets you digest everything about marketing on the world's largest online community. Facebook advertising seems like unknown territory to many marketers who feel as though they don't know their way around creating ads and managing them. Well, we hope that after reading this eBook, you will become a master in advertising.

All the strategies contained in this book are tested and trusted and are not merely author recommendations so it is a complete package of reliable ways to get your returns on investments while making sure that you do not incur unnecessary expenses for your ad campaigns. We have broken down all the intricacies of Facebook's great targeting options.

Although there are over 1.5 billion active users on the platform daily, Facebook has made it clear that they are focused on connecting users so businesses have to invest their time and money forget a chance to be among the top players in their respective fields. While you can avoid spending all your time on your Facebook Marketing campaign with automation options, you will have to be ready to put in financial resources to get yourself out there by paying for ads and sponsored posts. These are very important points in your campaign. Despite the fact that Facebook has every category of people that you need for your business, you may fail to make the best out of these numbers if you do not stick to the rules.

Finally, strategies, skills, tips, and tricks for Facebook Marketing are available to everyone who seeks to gain knowledge about it. This means that your competitors are also in search of ways to improve themselves to be the best in their industry. For everyone who seeks this knowledge, there is an ample amount of it waiting for them. You need to stay creative and unique with every strategy you choose to adopt. Above all, be convincing, for this is the only way your customer will choose you above your competition. Good luck!